ADVANCE PRAISE FOR

Punk Rockers' Revolution

"Fusing reflexive sociology, critique, and ethnography with hard data and personal narrative, Curry Malott and Milagros Peña offer a heartfelt dialogue that will extend our understanding of a nuanced and complex subculture. As oppositional subcultures mature, they are faced with tough challenges. The authors have addressed difficult questions rigorously and honestly. This work will advance and enliven what we know about social movements and the cultural process that underscores them."

—*Donna Gaines, Author of* Teenage Wasteland: Suburbia's Dead End Kids

Punk Rockers' Revolution

Studies in the Postmodern Theory of Education

Joe L. Kincheloe and Shirley R. Steinberg
General Editors

Vol. 223

PETER LANG
New York • Washington, D.C./Baltimore • Bern
Frankfurt am Main • Berlin • Brussels • Vienna • Oxford

Curry Malott + Milagros Peña

Punk Rockers' Revolution

A Pedagogy of Race, Class, and Gender

FOREWORD BY Rudolfo Chávez
AFTERWORD BY Peter McLaren
AND Jonathan Mclaren

PETER LANG
New York • Washington, D.C./Baltimore • Bern
Frankfurt am Main • Berlin • Brussels • Vienna • Oxford

Library of Congress Cataloging-in-Publication Data

Malott, Curry.
Punk rockers' revolution: a pedagogy of race, class, and gender /
Curry Malott and Milagros Peña.
p. cm. — (Counterpoints; v. 223)
Includes bibliographical references (p.).
1. Punk rock music—Social aspects. I. Peña, Milagros.
II. Title. III. Series: Counterpoints (New York, N.Y.); v. 223.
ML3918.R63M35 306.4'84—dc21 2002023813
ISBN 0-8204-6142-3
ISSN 1058-1634

Bibliographic information published by **Die Deutsche Bibliothek**.
Die Deutsche Bibliothek lists this publication in the "Deutsche Nationalbibliografie"; detailed bibliographic data is available on the Internet at http://dnb.ddb.de/.

Cover design by Lisa Barfield

The paper in this book meets the guidelines for permanence and durability of the Committee on Production Guidelines for Book Longevity of the Council of Library Resources.

275 Seventh Avenue, 28th Floor, New York, NY 10001
www.peterlangusa.com

Printed in the United States of America

We dedicate our efforts to Curry Malott's mom Sally Francis; his sisters Hannah Malott; Kristen Batch and her husband Greg Batch and their daughter Ruby; the love of his life, Jacquie Valencia; his grandparents Harold and Ruth Francis; dad Paul and aunt Sue Malott; cousins David, Eva, Hadd Francis, Susan James, her daughter Grace, and aunt Toni and uncle Sam Francis; cousins Jacob, Zachary and Alice Harlow and aunt Cathy and uncle Richard Harlow. Milagros Peña thanks her husband and partner in life Fred Hamann for continuing to enhance her appreciation for music as protest narratives. We also thank Marc Pruyn, Donna Gaines, Katlin Langston, Amy Lamb, Brandon Noland, Rami Krayem, Rusty Youngblood, Tate Rolofs, Jeff Taylor, Jon and Marty Musch, Joseph Carroll-Miranda, Danny "Kerse" Reyes, David Valencia, Blanca Cabrera, Rosemary Cabrera, Ramon Olivas, Gerardo Garcia, Angie Ronquillo and daughter Gia, Ray Padilla, Reed Elliot, Drikeena Smith, Adam from *The Dirt*, Stacy Duncan, Vince, Eva and Adriena Hernandez, Shirley Steinberg, Joe Kincheloe, Uli Elser, Jello Biafra, Greg Ginn, Anthony Couty, Nichole Fuch, Garrett Lamb, and their children Leo, and Allie, and so many others who have touched our lives, you know who you are. Finally, we would like to dedicate *Punk Rocker's Revolution* to the loving memory of Mike Taylor, Jason Hardenburger, and Derrick Whitesell, gone before their time.

Table of Contents

Tables

Acknowledgments

Grateful acknowledgment is hereby made to copyright holders for permission to use the following copyrighted material:

The Beatnigs, *Control*, 1988, Used by permission courtesy of Alternative Tentacles.

Dead Kennedys, *Holiday in Cambodia*, 1980, Used by permission courtesy of Decay Music.

Lard, *Generation Execute*, 1997, Used by permission courtesy of Alternative Tentacles.

Minutemen, *Just Another Soldier*, 1985, Used by permission courtesy of Cesstone Music.

Minutemen, *Paranoid Chant*, 1980, Used by permission courtesy of Cesstone Music.

NOMEANSNO, *Hunt the She Beast*, 1987, Used by permission courtesy of Alternative Tentacles.

Tribe 8, *Butch in the Streets*, 1995, Used by permission courtesy of Alternative Tentacles.

Tribe 8, *Flippersnapper,* 1995, Used by permission courtesy of Alternative Tentacles.

Tribe 8, *Mendo Hoo-Ha*, 1997, Used by permission courtesy of Alternative Tentacles.

Tribe 8, *Wrong Bathroom*, 1996, Used by permission courtesy of Alternative Tentacles.

Wesley Willis, *Chronic Schizophrenia*, 1995, Used by permission courtesy of Alternative Tentacles.

Foreword

As a boy growing up on a farm, along with all sorts of farm animals, chickens, turkeys, pigs, horses, and milk cows, we had several working dogs. I have a fondness for working dogs, big or small—the kind that will watch over a wrench accidentally dropped in the middle of a plowed field after tightening up some bolts on a tractor plow. Or the dog that gives that special bark so you know someone unknown is approaching. So when the January 2002 edition of *National Geographic* magazine cover story on the evolution of dogs was published, I was interested. I did not think that this same story would serve to illustrate the importance of *Punk Rockers' Revolution: Pedagogy of Gender, Race, and Class* to education in general and to critical studies in particular.

More times than not, *National Geographic* will strike at the social dynamics of informationalism (Castells 1998) never wanting to offend the many that simply "like the pictures." The particular article in the January 2002 *National Geographic* captures the indispensability of dogs to our human evolution. Ironically, the article also captures how a "dog's life" can compare to the actual plight of people from around the world flagrantly minimized by the neoliberal consumption the following depicts. On page sixteen there is a picture of a Maltese named "Tiffy" atop her ottoman with the caption noting that the dog "leads a plush life on Manhattan's Upper East Side [and is] cared for like a baby." The description is telling:

> In her Park Avenue apartment on New York's Upper East Side, NancyJane Loewy feeds Tiffy, her fluffy, eight-pound Maltese, twice a day from an enviable larder. Along with her dog food, says Loewy, "I'll give her a little chicken for breakfast, some steamed baby carrots, steamed broccoli, and some sweet potato—a balanced diet. For dinner I might add lamb or steak or poached salmon or tuna with steamed vegetables. And for dessert some low-fat yogurt with no sugar, maybe just a teaspoon of strawberry or apricot yogurt to sweeten it, and a couple of red grapes sliced in half. Then I'll give her one or two Teddy Grahams, she likes those, and maybe some Pepperidge Farm Goldfish crackers for snacks (p. 16).

Juxtapose this "act" of consumption with the summation by the ICFI-based (International Committee of the Fourth International) on the World Health Organization and United Nations reports of the late 1990s:

> ›nsumption has expanded at an unprecedented pace over the twentieth ..ury, with private and public consumption expenditures reaching $24 trillion in 1998, twice the level of 1975 and six times that of 1950. Consumption per capita has increased steadily in industrialized countries (about 2.3 percent annually over the past 25 years). In contrast, the poorest 20 percent of the world's population have been left out of the consumption explosion. The average African household, for instance, consumes 20 percent less than it did 25 years ago. Well over one billion people are deprived of basic consumption needs. Of the 4.4 billion people in the oppressed countries, nearly three-fifths lack basic sanitation. Almost a third have no access to clean water. One-quarter do not have adequate housing. A fifth have no access to modern health services and do not have enough dietary energy and protein. A fifth of children do not attend school to grade 5. Worldwide 2.2 billion people are anemic, including 55 million in industrialized countries. In the oppressed countries, only a privileged minority has access to motorized transport, telecommunications and modern energy. (Kent 1998, http://www.wsws.org/news/1998/sep1998/pov-s23.shtml, accessed October 10, 2003).

Punk Rockers' Revolution is a self-examination of what we are as a society, and to a great degree, what we have accepted through our own complicit blindness to the social dynamics of informationalism; what Manuel Castells has poignantly labeled as the social differentiation of *inequality*, *polarization*, *poverty*, and *misery* (1998). Mournfully captured by the above polarized examples of consumption is the backdrop of what makes this volume an indispensable tool for a teacher such as myself, whose ears, dispositions, and unconscious biases do not listen to  or care to listen to (until now) and understand the primal urges for moral clarity that punk rock many times can provide. Malott and Peña do not argue that punk rock is a social movement, but they do show that it can be part of a  struggle for justice and humanization.

Unlike the 1970s' and 1980s' legacies of a skaterpunkhippiehiphopper that Curry Malott courageously speaks to with all self-revealing contradictions or the U.S. Dominican's "take" on Jim Crow à la NYC via the rock and roll protest songs that Milagro Peña's "heart burnings" show, my understanding of their world is contextualized to the sounds of Malo, Azteca, Tortilla Factory, Chicano, War, and La Nueva Canción of the 1970s. Fearful but not reluctant were my feelings as I accepted the writing of this foreword. A genre of ignorance masked in petulant ignorance and unfounded fear were my initial uncoverings as I read, enjoyed, learned, and reflected on this critical volume. Through their analyses, both quantitative and qualitative, *Punk Rockers' Revolution* moved me to continue peeling the onion of oppression within me, to see anew that which I signified wrongfully as noise, and to reconsider the rawness of the many oppressions I have intellectualized. How unnerving and embarrassing it was for me to realize that the new protest song of social and economic justice could take root in what appears as the cliché of undiscipline and mayhem (i.e., "head banger music"). Punk rock is "*la nueva canción*"—the new protest song of today. Arising from the streets of disenfranchisement and the byways of hypocrisy, *Punk Rockers' Revolution* is a metacognitive tool for teachers of all kinds to humanize what may have manifest as bias-filled images of the Other—unconsciously cast through one's prejudice of what music should be. *Punker Rockers' Revolution* is another dialogical tool needed by teachers in the thick of learning with learners to demystify that which we must connect to "common experience rooted in societies marked by [and for] exploitation and alienation" (Malott & Peña, this volume, p. 60).

In *Punk Rockers' Revolution: Pedagogy of Gender, Race, and Class*, Curry Malott and Milagro Peña position themselves to expressively show that punk rock uncovers what are still, sadly, fat times with Reaganesque zeal drenched in globalized, neoliberal obsessions of reducing societies to economies, economies to markets, and markets to financial flows (Castells 1998). Malott and Peña show that even though punk rock can be and is phobic, racist, and misogynist it is also revolutionary, antifascist, anti-violence, antiracist, profeminist, procreative, and against ignorance.

With astuteness and with all glorified presumptions of punkers aside, Malott and Peña strip punk rock of what many times has been perceived as rudeness by insightfully addressing its contradictions and hyperbole, proceeding to create a story, raw as it may seem, but so in need of telling. There are a growing handful of punkers out there willing to engage the discourse of slander of the human condition in the name of profits, consumption, and male and gender supremacy by reflecting and critiquing that which so many of us have internalized. And, in turn, Malott and Peña argue, this conscientization will lead to social action and ultimately social change. It is the conscious analysis of this story that makes it so special. In *Cultural Action for Freedom*, Freire (1970a) speaks to a consciousness that resonates well throughout *Punk Rockers' Revolution.*

> Consciousness is never a mere reflection of, but a reflection upon, material reality....If it is true that consciousness is impossible without the world which constitutes it, it is equally true that this world is impossible if the world itself, in constituting consciousness, does not become an object of its critical reflection (p. 29).

...ott and Peña in this book rightly argue that as beings of praxis, punk rockers are, by their acts of transforming the world through music, song, and personal actions, humanizing our world. Punk rockers have this potential, even if, as Freire argues (1970a), the unmasking that can liberate us to become more human may not yet signify the humanization of oneself or others. Malott and Peña state:

> The critical awareness that we speak of, results in embracing all of our differences as representative of the human condition—that is, as creative cultural producers—in order to build alliances and new social movements that transcend borders, however we define them. Despite the seeming differences in punk rock messages, punk rock sits squarely among those new social movements that look for ways to build bridges among potential political allies against common enemies—capitalism, fascism, racism, and sexism to name a few. And like so many other movements, punk rock is a product of the social criticism of its time (p. 61).

Punk rockers know and intuit whom the economy of consumption privileges. "In 1998, the last year for which figures from the Federal Reserve Board are available, the top one percent owned 47.3 percent of financial wealth" (Domhoff 2003, 64). "If the upper ten percent is considered, it has 90 percent" of the wealth (Domhoff 2003, 64). Despite all the talk of trickle down economics, wealth at these levels "has not been concentrated since 1929" (Domhoff 2003, 64).

This same control of wealth and what many punk rockers see and sing to their audiences is what makes them so unpalatable to the status quo. Malott and Peña remind us that in the early 1990s between "8 and 12 multinational corporations controlled 80% of all mass media, television, newspapers, radio, movies, music, in other words, everything" (p. 151). The cultural spaces punk rock occupies are now more than ever in the history of the music industry controlled to reproduce the "Stepford" domesticities so many of us have grown to see as normal. Although Malott and Peña point out that punk rock is and continues to be loud, repetitive, simple, angry, white, male, and against society, they have shown that it is much more: "punk rock is fluid and historically contingent, best characterized as a cultural space rather than as musical style. It is no longer just one style, but a place, one of the only places, [they argue] where groups and individuals with varying styles can express ideas and tell stories that would not be heard otherwise" (p. 154). *Punk Rockers' Revolution* is a tool for self-examination of our feelings of anxiety we deny that poverty, racism, and sexism are all around us. *Punk Rockers' Revolution* is a tool to affirm the emptiness and meaninglessness we have come to deny within ourselves as evidenced by the metaphorical Tiffys we accept and call cute in Fifth Avenues around the world, when just down the street people are hungry and are dying on the streets; *Punk Rockers' Revolution* names that which so many of us have refused to accept, much less name, in an increasingly capitalist, hostile, violent, racist, and sexist world. *Punk Rockers' Revolution* creates a space for allies to commune in dialog through and about a musical genre that can be the new song of protest in neoliberal times when an unrelenting disregard of shame comforts us like a warm Tiffy in a plush Fifth Avenue apartment.

Rudolfo Chávez Chávez, Professor
Curriculum and Instruction
College of Education
New Mexico State University

Chapter 1
The Bias in Our Study: Who We Are, Where We Come from, and This Study

> Do you remember Being the first punk in town/ Outlaw #1/ For the t-shirt you had on. Now you stay home/ Mad at the whole scene/ For refusing to freeze in 1983…
>
> Jello Biafra (with MoJo Nixon), "Nostalgia for an Age That Never Existed," excerpt from the album *Prairie Home Invasion*, Alternative Tentacles 1993.

Curry Malott: My First Ten in Ohio

My Northern European knowledge base was passed on to me in the land of the woodland's tribes (e.g., the Miami) of the Ohio valley where much of my family has lived for generations. Through genocide, cultural genocide, and other "removal programs," European colonization transformed (is transforming) this land into an urban/rural wasteland including Dayton, Ohio, where much of my family lives. My middle-working class, "white" (mostly German and British) family helped socialize me into thinking in dichotomies and understanding the world and our communities as "contested-terrain" (Edwards 1979), good and evil, marked by the division between working people and governments/ corporations. My experiences in Dayton showed me the injustices created by capitalism and dominant society's use of racism, sexism, and classism to construct conceptions of good and evil in a city occupied by large populations of Africans and Europeans. Such strategies are used to divide working people, to sustain capitalist interests, and to confuse the boundaries between oppressors and oppressed. In the words of the contemporary African American revolutionary, Dhoruba Bin Wahad, in *Still Black, Still Strong: Survivors of the War Against Black Revolutionaries* (1993):

> Racism has been an important tool in dividing the poor and working peoples of America. It has prevented white laborers, the middle-class, and various Third World immigrant communities from uniting against an exploitative and relatively small white male elite (p. 71).

My granddad once told me, as we drove through an abandoned neighborhood of old steel factories in Dayton, that race relations were far less tense when he was a much younger man—when relatively "good" factory jobs were more abundant in the area. An abundance of jobs and the subsequent low levels of unemployment puts workers in such a context in a position of relative power in relation to their capitalist overseers, as they tend to be less desperate for work and with more to bargain with. Making sense of this phenomena Alex Callinicos (1993) argues that "white" workers tend to become more susceptible to racist ideology when the working-class is in a position of low power, and thus ineffective at struggling for higher wages and better working conditions, in relation to the capitalist class. On the other hand, when workers are in a position of high power in relation to the capitalist class, they are more apt to have faith in their ability to work with their brothers and sisters of color, and thus less susceptible to racism. As corporations began to realize that the workers' unions could be co-opted and used to do what the state and capital had been unable to do, that is, discipline the workers, unions almost instantly became officially sanctioned. Discipline was guaranteed through such tactics as taking away what many have argued is working peoples' most powerful weapon against capital, the strike, and replacing it with "the contract" (Berry et al. 1974; Kloby 1999). Such actions were done in the name of "national interest" because, it was argued, it is in the nation's interest to have a large rate of production, and thus it is imperative to keep working at whatever cost.

Eventually large numbers of jobs disappeared as corporations sought out cheaper labor south of the border (i.e., Mexico)—a process known as *corporate flight*. Life for working-class whites in Ohio and elsewhere changed, and when they turned to blame someone they turned to beliefs they had internalized, taught to them by a dominant white society, which promoted myths of those "lazy blacks," "Mexicans," and "welfare mothers"—ideas readily accessible as worker power decreased, a trend yet unchanged. *They* were the causes of their problems not greedy corporations, unions, and procapital/antidemocratic governments.

By the early 1970s the backlash against the social gains made during the 1920s and the 1960s in the labor movement was well under way. In my granddad's case, he became very antigovernment, anticapital, and antiunion accusing them all of being "crooks," "liars," "criminals," and "thugs." Largely because of his white-skinned privilege, and his skills and ability, my granddad has managed to survive remodeling houses for relatively well-off white folks. My granddad has taught me, yet not without contradictions, valuable lessons, pushing me to find and fulfill my dream for a positive, strong, active, antiracist society.

When I was growing up, some of my closest family members, like my dad's sister and my mom's brother, still lived in parts of industrial Dayton where "white" and "black" working-class neighborhoods overlapped, which was (and is) thick with racial tension during the 1980s when I was coming of age. More recently, these neighborhoods have become more African American and more oppressed.

Through my years of public schooling during weekend and summer visits to my cousin's house situated in the heart of these Dayton, Ohio, working-class neighborhoods, one of my male cousins, five years my elder, served as one of my most influential teachers and antiracist role models. When we were kids, he showed me how he survived in the city where our labor power was not worth as much as it was just ten years earlier. Avoiding the cops and "getting jumped," as well as shoplifting and using government services (like the summer lunch programs), in retrospect, seemed to be common tactics of surviving in the city as a youth. What power *was/is* available to the youth (other than the white-privilege available to some, which most are not cognizant of; Tatum 1997) was/is in collective creativity, the "symbolic" in relation to the dominant society—a power negotiated in the everyday lives of youth in and out of the classroom.

When we were kids, my older cousin did not assume the white racist stance common to many whites of our community as much as many of us. Instead, from where I stood, it seemed that he attempted to assume a more creative, hybrid stance as he walked and experienced life *with* some of his African American classmates and neighbors. However, my cousin always maintained his white, middle-class–influenced dialect common to the academy, giving him intellectual credibility throughout his schooling experience often earning 4.0 grade point averages, shedding light on the issues of cultural capital associated with the disparate push-out rates among whites, African Americans and Latinas/os (McLaren, 1989).

Such insight regarding culture and power showed me the value and necessity of a cultural revolution in the here and now (avoiding "nostalgia for an age that never existed"), and in particular the value of having the ability to create identities capable of moving between and within the overlapping realities of our collective communities. In doing so there is a rich history of youth creating new, hybrid, resistant identities in the face of an oppressive, divide-and-rule, dominant system.

However, within such subversive, resistant stances, including the punk stances central to this project, has embodied elements of internalized oppression, which, as a result of my ongoing participation, has been passed on to me. That is, a drug-induced, self-destructiveness that spirals with cynicism and with age as ideas from the dominant society invade our consciousness and old friends from the neighborhood find themselves locked up—physically and/or mentally buried. Our resistance was often used by the dominant society to turn us into cogs for the prison system if you resisted society's norms, increasing the pressure on those of us not caught up in the game to conform to the dominant ideology. Instead they created cynical, bitter people who have long since given up hope for a better future freed from the constraints of capital and its divisive tendencies such as racism. My family, on the other hand, provided me with not only both oppressive normative, but with alternative ways of thinking. They also gave me much needed love. They supported me through my experiences in school as a "learning disabled student."

Privilege in Context

Both of my parents are the first in their families to go to college and get doctoral degrees, and both fit within current boundaries of whiteness and as whites, receive white-privilege. Some of my cousins, however, do not benefit from white, *middle-class* privilege, and unfortunately, there has not been a complete absence of class-based tension within the family. For the most part, despite the working-class status of my extended family and the years I spent doing manual labor, including restaurant work, my life has been riddled with white-privilege, all of it made possible by a dominant society that has given me privilege through not only colonization, slavery, and the continued exploitation and oppression of people of color, and women in particular, but through the very creation of "whiteness" (Feagin & Vera 1995).

Thus my oppression is relative, and as a young boy who, more so than others in my extended family, fit within boundaries of whiteness, with some middle-class status in school as a result of my parents earning Ph.D.s, I benefited from many institutionalized privileges. Aside from my learning-disabled status in school and the pressure of life in an imperialist, supremacist, capitalist society, most of the oppression I have experienced in my life is a result of how I was socialized by my family and community. Consequently, rejecting racism and sexism and fighting economic exploitation are choices I have made, like others, by joining (re-creating) and building (creating) subversive communities of resistance like punk rock, the focus of this study.

I came of age during the conservative 1980s when what I call the humane-deficient, dominant society, led by *republicrats* (Republicans + Democrats) Ronald Reagan and George Bush, staged a war on women, people of color, and working people in general, employing the methods of trickle-down economics that tax the poor and give to the rich. The 1980s was a reactionary period, a response to the political gains made by social movements of the 1960s and 1970s. The arguments used to sell trickle-down economics to U.S. voters was that increasing the wealth of the rich will not make them greedier but will make them more humane and create more jobs, trickling the increased productivity downward and thus increasing the wealth of working people. This is not what happened. The increased wealth of the rich has not trickled down. Instead, corporations have abandoned many "too costly" U.S. workers and have moved many factory jobs south of the U.S.–Mexico border, where they are getting away with paying below subsistence wages. Many new U.S. jobs, on the other hand, have expanded in the service industry (in places like McDonalds and Wal-Mart), further ghettoizing into low-paying industries working people in general, particularly traditionally middle-class people.

As a white, middle-/working-class male, I benefit from the material objects produced within this thinly veiled system of slavery. As a white male, I have not been the direct target of racist or sexist policies or practices, though life in a racist society suppresses the humanity of all. Of course those who are oppressed are dehumanized, but those who oppress themselves cannot fully be human (Freire 1970b). Indeed, my life has been hurt (in ways I'm probably still unaware of) as a result of living in an oppressive, dehumanizing society.

Uprooted and Off to Oregon

After the first ten years of my life in Ohio, my mother got a teaching job at Oregon State University and moved my two sisters and me to Corvallis, Oregon. It was there I used the knowledge handed down to me by my family and community to organize, create community, resist, and take on, at times, a self-destructive stance. Carrying the label of "learning disabled" with me to Corvallis, I sought out new communities as an adolescent/youth.

I found and helped create a new community in the lower middle-/working-class neighborhood we moved into—the neighborhood my mom still lives in to this day. My first friends were the outcasts, the cast aside—what Karl Marx called the lumpen-proletariat—the undesirables, those who deviated most from what the power structure considered normal and smart, the white, middle-class, heterosexual, conservative male. The idea for this new family, although we didn't verbalize it as such, was and is an ever-changing and expanding network of people united around similar and often contradictory ideas about justice and about being in the world. Specifically, we took and continue to take resistant stances toward the roles the humane-deficient, dominant-oppressor culture attempts to prescribe for us. This stance is a uniting, revolutionary, although often self-destructive, stance. There are prescribed roles for all of us, as blacks, as whites, as Latinos, as men, as women, as workers, as bosses, and so forth, which we all create and re-create, resist and accommodate. The difference in the conscious resistant stance that other punkers and I propose is that the conscious resistance is preceded by a consciousness of the oppressor-conditioned mindset—that is—how we develop "critical consciousness" (Freire 1970b).

The process by which critical consciousness, resistance, and revolutionary stances are constructed emerges: the praxis (theory and practice) of taking a resistant stance toward what we understand as unjust and oppressive, not only to ourselves but to others, is particularly important to me as a man of privilege. I attempt to destroy the whiteness within myself not just because it oppresses me, but because it oppresses others. My closest friends have always had great senses of humor, but have also been the most self-destructive. At the same time, my friends have been and have become the crustiest, rudest punks, the hardest head-bangers, the baddest b-boys, the most serious Gangstas, the craziest *cholos*, and the most radical academics. In short, as a result, my attempted commitment to social justice throughout most of my life came from what I have been taught from these people who are the most resistant, and who have taken, in my view, very potentially revolutionary stances.

It is important to stress, however, that becoming more aware of our conditioned consciousness does not mean that our attempts at creating new, more humane, revolutionary cultures will be free of all the oppressive ideas of any given humane-deficient, dominant society. According to Paulo Freire (1970b), it is through permanent and cultural revolution as a process that we can re-create society. Through dialogue we can weed out the oppressive ideologies of the oppressor (i.e., whiteness, patriarchy, heterosexism, capitalism, etc.) that we have internalized as a result of being conditioned by society in our ideas and actions.

Adding to those other things mentioned, my cousin taught me to live my life not *for* but *with* the Other, enabling me to detect contradictory and oppressive ideas of the dominant society within myself and society at large. Like my cousin in Ohio, in Oregon I too lived my life *with* the Other. My first friend in Oregon, Johny Taylor, was one of the only African American kids in our elementary school, Fair Play. Johny lived in what we called the red roof apartments, which were housing projects a couple blocks from my mom's house. We met my first year in Oregon in the fifth grade, and were both from single-mother families. One day at school in detention Johny and I, two fifth-grade boys, talked seriously about running away to California, away from all the bullshit we got for both being and not being who we were prescribed to be. Instead of running away we resisted, built communities, and self-destructed.

Feeling and being treated as outcasts of society, we constructed our own norms and values according to our sense of justice, as a form of survival and resistance. Collectively facing institutionalized racism, economic exploitation, and repression from school and the community at large, we created different norms and values from the dominant society essential for our sense of self-worth and survival. However socialization is a powerful force, and our resistance was often filled with self-hate, thus taking the form of self-destruction. Destructive not because we resisted what little our schools had to offer, as many theorists suggest (Willis 1977; McLaren 1989; Shor 1992), but because in the process of destroying our prescribed roles, we too often destroyed and destroy ourselves. Unable to reach higher levels of critical consciousness, our denouncement of our present reality and the announcement of a new, more just reality, rarely leads to new action and reflection (Freire 1970b).

One of the reasons we often fail to reach higher levels of critical consciousness might be a result of our inability to connect with our past in a way that can change our present and future. Quite often, in destroying our prescribed roles we try to forget or reinvent our histories, failing to acknowledge that the creation of a better, not-yet-materialized reality depends on our ability to openly and honestly critically reflect on our histories as a way of situating our own lives in a broader historical context that would give us the ability to name it for what it really is. In taking this approach we come to know better where we want to go and not go. For example, after my mom moved my sisters and me to Oregon and I began gaining distance from the university community in Oxford, Ohio, where I was first given the label "learning disabled," I began to dissociate myself from that community, leaving those experiences out of my life story. I now realize that a critical understanding of those experiences, which included much of the first ten years of my life, is central to my understanding of where I have been, where I am, and where I am going.

Wrestling with the struggle to make sense of the world and to create a more just society, many of us fall down from time to time, and some of us stay down. Too often we fight and kill each other instead of the source of our oppression. Johny, for example, has been in and out of prison for gang-related crimes, including attempted manslaughter. Getting caught in the system in this way is exactly what the dominant society wants. In addition, a number of us become drug addicts and/or alcoholics. Many of us have committed suicide. Some of us have turned to hate groups like Nazi skinheads. We often use each other for sex, which manifests itself as sexism when men use their sexual power to control women, and many of us direct our rage at homosexuality in homophobic fits of violence. Much of this destructiveness is a result of the negative messages about ourselves we internalize through the humane-deficient, dominant society's cultural institutions such as schools, which serve to divide and rule over us (Freire 1970b). But we are not the criminals. We do not have an institutionalized voice in the social construction of criminality, although through unconscious consent we too often support what the humane-deficient, dominant society defines as "criminal." Those with not only institutionalized privilege, and those with institutionalized power through the power of corporations, engage in the act of what Sabina Virgo (1996) calls the "criminalization of poverty." Those who exploit working people do not define their own activities as criminal. Through the social institutions we encounter in our everyday lives, we receive subtle and not so subtle messages that it is not criminal to exploit and enslave people, but it is criminal to play rap music, to be black or brown, to be a skaterpunk, or to be poor. This is what many of us are told and kids are taught.

During my life in schools in Oregon, I connected with middle-class skaters and poor white punks and hippies, and drew heavily on heavy metal and punk rock music and styles of dress. Johny drew on black Gangstas, and hip-hop for music and style. Together we constructed our own potentially revolutionary, hybrid codes and styles. Unlike Johny, however, who was pushed out of our high school by his sophomore year, my white, middle-class male privilege helped get me involved with the university, giving me distance from my communities. My endeavors at the university have led me to read multicultural, radical, revolutionary, education theories. These theoretical perspectives gave me the tools to reach a level of critical consciousness that enabled me to become the ever-changing skaterpunkhippiehiphopper, middle-class academic that is capable of identifying destructive and oppressive ideas within oneself and society at large. It is who I am today.

Through never-ending dialogue, reflection, and action I negotiate and renegotiate places and spaces within the cultural terrain of this society. As a result of my decision to stand next to those I do, and by rejecting being a hard-working, conservative, white boy the system wants me to be, I experience the prejudices and violence that are conditioned responses directed at those who do not passively accept their roles. This is the space from which I write this piece—through the lens of a critically conscious, anticapital, privileged, academic, in process, skaterpunkhippiehiphopper who was raised as a white male during the conservative 1980s in Ohio and Oregon. In this sojourn, my life crossed paths with teachers so unlike others I had before, from a world so different than mine. Milagros (Milly) Peña, the second author of this book and I met while I was a student at New Mexico State University. Later Milly, in her own words, remarks on what she brings to our discussion of punk, but suffice it to say that her teaching, mentoring, and friendship is part of what we argue here creates possibilities for much-needed genuine dialogue across race, class, and gender.

The Study in Context for Curry Malott

This is part of my history of being an active participant in the world, which affects why I look for like-minded people, and read words and the world the way I do. According to the epistemology of scientific theory, it constitutes the biased perspective from which I write and think, which is important to know, for "there can be no observation without an observer" (Corrigan 1989, 68). I am wholeheartedly dedicated to underground countercultures and anticapitalist struggles, yet feel it is an increasingly hard struggle to resist my ever-changing prescribed societal roles, and so I work to maintain an organic, in the Gramscian sense described in Chapter 4 (pp. 61-64), connectedness to the punk world. By doing this piece I am extending my protest venue. It is my purpose in this study, to act as an "organic intellectual," connecting communities I belong to, by situating myself in institutions of higher education, the object of much of my resistant stance, or as Philip Corrigan (1989) in postmodern terms puts it, taking a stance of "refusal."

Milagros Peña: New Yorker, Latina, from a Working Poor Family

Unlike Curry Malott, I grew up in New York's inner city, born to working poor Latino parents. Having come to the United States from the Dominican Republic as teenagers, one parent never finished grammar school and the other dropped out of high school to go to work. America's Dream for Obtacilio Peña

Tejada (my father) and Milagros Martínez López (my mother) was a delusion. By the time my parents passed away, one from alcoholism and the other from brain cancer after years of prescription drugs to treat schizophrenia and depression, what my parents achieved after a lifetime of struggle was embodied in their children. I'm the first Ph.D. in my family. My parents' struggles are embodied in what I choose to write and how I came to this book project.

I came of age in New York City in the late 1960s and early 1970s, during the civil rights movements of the 1960s, the Vietnam War, and the War on Poverty. But the conservative backlash that began with Richard Nixon in the early 1970s (described earlier by Curry) and extends into the present have conspired to dash our hopes to create a more fair and just society. My experiences growing up provided the context for my exposure to racism, class warfare, and sexism. In the 1960s I saw my first role model get drafted to Vietnam. Some thought we should be comforted because the marines were better than losing my uncle to the streets and to gangs. While some sang protest songs against the war and the loss of four students at Kent State in Ohio, my family clung to the television, waited for mail, and hoped that my uncle and his street friends would all come back alive. My uncle came back; some of his friends didn't. From my perspective, my family fled the Dominican Republic's U.S.–backed dictator Trujillo and his reign of terror over my family and the Dominican people just to find us exposed to another mess the United States had created, except now in Asia.

My introduction to protest music came with my resonating with the lyrics of the 1960s and 1970s, particular those songs that focused on the horrors of war, poverty, and racism. Though my family came from another country, they quickly learned about Jim Crow when my father, barely speaking English, was drafted into the army to fight North Koreans, and as a mixed-race Latino had to drink out of water fountains designated for coloreds while stationed at the army base in Fayetteville, North Carolina, in the early 1950s. He then came home only to find that despite service to his country, he, like African Americans, couldn't live just anywhere in New York City. Jim Crow was manifested in preserving color lines in northern U.S. cities, and just as in the south, there were consequences if those color lines were crossed. That is how we came to settle in New York City's first Dominican neighborhood, on Manhattan Avenue between 100th and 109th streets. So when whites feared the visits of Malcolm X to New York City's Harlem, not too far from where we lived, we listened, though feared the retaliation of a city that openly and shamelessly practiced racism. When Malcolm X and Martin Luther King Jr. were murdered, members

! other local autonomy movements, are connected to the shifting ...daries between public, private, and social life. "They involve struggles against old and new forms of domination" (Cohen & Arato 1992, 516), as we argue is present in punk protest. What is new in these social movement strategies is an appreciation for an activism that goes beyond critiques of oppressive social institutions as abstractions, but goes after challenges to transform normative expectations of individual behavior, beliefs, and values. We also borrow on other theoretical perspectives that are used here to understand further the punk phenomenon. What follows in Chapter 2 is a discussion of punk rock via these broader theoretical lenses (pp. 15-40).

The Focus of Our Study

The focus of this study is on a small but important aspect of our struggle for social change. We focus on the lyrical stances of recorded punk rock voices, specifically the content of the music on three punk rock record labels. The import of this study lies in identifying and contributing to a general epistemological direction for a small part of our struggle. Put another way, the general question guiding this study is: How has and is punk rock serving to combat capitalist domination and its use of racism, classism, and sexism to thwart communities of protest? As a result of doing this study, we amplify some of the marginalized Others' voices and the perspectives (stances) of a heterogeneous group of individuals connected by a common stance, here as punk rocker. In addition, by focusing not only on resistant aspects of punk rock but on accommodative, self-destructive aspects as well, this study contributes to the advancement of punk rock as a potentially revolutionary countercapitalist stance.

For punk rockers, music and art have often been used as tools of both resisting and accommodating the interests of the dominant classes. During the late 1970s a predominantly white, .male, working-/middle-class counterculture now known as punk rock began to develop. The purpose of this study is to show how punk rock has served both to subvert and accommodate the interests of late-capitalist U.S. society by looking at the trends in the ideas, values, and beliefs transmitted through lyrical messages and how it has evolved over time. Applying content analysis, a method of analysis we use in this study, allows you to study patterns of words and phrases in music lyrics. In this book we pay particular attention to: (1) who punk rockers have been traditionally and who they are today, and (2) what messages they promoted and continue to promote as the music evolved since the late 1970s as part of the punk community's struggle for social change.

Chapter 2
Class-Based Theories of Popular Culture

Punk rock as a subcultural-youth-stance can be understood in Marxist and neo-Marxist terms, despite the fact that historically popular culture has not been given significant attention in the discourse of the Left or of the Right (Giroux & Simon 1989). The following will briefly outline Marxist and neo-Marxist perspectives on education in order to demonstrate how they offer different ways of interpreting popular culture, specifically punk rock as a musical phenomenon. We also focus on the way ideas of resistance in postmodern terms have perceived popular subcultures and interpreted punk rock. In addition, we provide our own narrative on how resistance theory and postmodernism can be used to interpret how punk rock reproduces dominant ideologies, while at the same time producing its own subversive, resistant, counter capitalist, potentially revolutionary ideologies. In doing so, we develop our own interpretations and along with cultural theories develop a better way to understand punk rock.

Marxism and Culture

In his writings Marx did not deal directly with the issue of culture and its role in the production and reproduction of capitalist society. Marx did, however, briefly discuss education and its role in reproducing class structures. Because Marx's writings specifically on education are not extensive, contemporary Marxist writers focus on "Marx's analysis of social dynamics to develop their ideas regarding the role of education in a base/superstructure dialectic" (Armaline et al. 1994, 178).

Marx saw the relations of production as the primary driving force in society, which are affected by and affect the material relations of production that change with technological advancements. But customs and laws perpetuate status quo relations because, according to Marx, they are highly resistant to change. In their class struggles, individuals fight for control and, ultimately, power over the state and the hearts and minds of its citizens. In this struggle, control over education becomes an important factor. Schools reproduce social class, the next work force, and teach the children of the lower classes that capitalism works for everyone. Highlighted in many writings, including *The Communist Manifesto 1848* (1964), Marx and Engels believed that the working class would eventually gain control of their own schools as an inevitable consequence of the natural historical development of human existence.

In *The Communist Manifesto,* Marx and Engels state that "the history of all hitherto existing society is the history of class struggles" (1964, 57). Marx and Engels believed that the natural course of history would result in the replacement of capitalism with socialism, which they saw as a natural absolute good that transcends time and culture. Left out of Marx's perspective was what Brazilian Educator Paulo Freire (1970b) later expressed as the very essence of being human—the ability to act in and (re-)create reality through culture, and to be in the world not just as a participant of history but as creators of history. In this light, revolution and societal transformation is not just an inevitable result of history but an objective reality organized by people conscious of their own consciousness and drawing on their creative abilities mediated by particular historical objective material conditions. The works of Paulo Freire, which we return to later, are informed by a number of theorists and revolutionaries, including Antonio Gramsci, a member of the Italian parliament and general secretary of the Communist Party during the 1920s. While in prison, where he died, Gramsci wrote extensively on the capitalist system's use of cultural institutions to indoctrinate society in favor of elite interests, and thus argues that the role culture needed to play was promoting the working class's struggle to transform capitalist societies.

Gramsci and Culture

Like Marx, Gramsci believed that schools act as mechanisms of ideological control (1929–1935, 1971). Unlike Marx, Gramsci, as well as other neo-Marxist theorists of the 1920s and 1930s, believed that schools in capitalist societies have the potential to be liberating institutions if the oppressed classes gain control of them. Gramsci held that the working class must obtain control of the cultural institutions used by the dominant society to exert and maintain control over the whole society. These elites' hegemonic grip on schools had to be challenged before the masses could begin to gain control of the state and ultimately economic production.

For Gramsci (1971) hegemony encapsulated the ideas, values, and beliefs of the dominant society that are transmitted through society's cultural institutions, in particular schools, media, organized religion, and government. From birth individuals internalize the ideas, values, and beliefs of the dominant society as natural and normal, and ultimately consent to their own domination without knowing it or believing that they can do anything about it. Through ideological indoctrination they are led to believe that hard work and determination lead to material success. By this view, poor people are failures; lazy products of their cultures of poverty. Yet when we look at the distribution of wealth in the United States, it becomes apparent given the forces of race, class, and gender discrimination that the culture of poverty argument does not hold up. For the culture of poverty theory to work, we would have to believe that value and intellect is naturally determined and that whites are superior to minorities. In believing so, we would have to ignore the practices and policies of European colonization in the Americas, including the legal and social privileges given to Euroethnics because of the color of their skin (Zinn 1980; 1997). We would have to ignore U.S. labor history and how a few became rich by exploiting advantages they gained through class privilege, and that until not too long ago women could not own property or vote. In such a state of denial, we would also have to forget how capitalism creates the environment where "The rich rob the poor and the poor rob each other" (Sojourner Truth quoted in Abu-Jamal 2000, 207). In other words, hegemony operates at the level of consent (Gramsci 1971). Capitalism works because marginalized people internalize their oppressions.

Therefore, the only solution is creating the possibility for counter hegemonic action where dominant cultural institutions can be transformed (Gramsci 1971). In the United States, counterhegemonic traditions of resistance and struggle emerged in the American Indian Movement, the Black Panther Party, the Socialist Workers Party and, we argue, among skaterpunks, to name a few examples. Gramsci (1971) described the leaders of these types of struggles for liberation as *organic intellectuals.* This is leadership that emerges from the protest community and appeals to a knowledge and culture based in the protest community and not necessarily shaped by schooling or formal training in the traditional sense. In our description of punk rockers as organic intellectuals, we describe a community of protestors, as they would say not known for their particular jobs, like medical doctors, lawyers, professors, and others viewed by society as those who encapsulate the best society produces.

Instead punk rockers are garbage collectors, factory workers, McDonalds' employees, and so forth. They are known and supported by others in their own community for conceptualizing the ideas and aspirations of the working-class communities they organically belong to (Gramsci 1971). Their purpose is to mediate their class's struggles and provide links with certain parts of the traditional intellectual community (i.e., universities). For example, according to Dancis (1978), working-class punk bands in England, such as Sham 69, have made links with the Socialist Workers Party (politically active traditional intellectuals), which resulted in "a group called 'Rock Against Racism' (RAR) whose goal is to fight the influences of racism and fascism in rock music" (p. 60). Yet rather than focusing on the counterhegemonic aspects of popular culture, which is the focus of this study, many neo-Marxist cultural theorists focus on the oppressive aspects of popular culture.

For example, like Gramsci, Theodor Adorno and Max Horkheimer of the Institute for Social Research at the University of Frankfurt have put blame on the role of popular culture and the state as perpetuators of oppressive ideology. According to Giroux and Simon, by these standards, popular culture "is simply mass culture whose effects have no redeeming political possibilities" (1989, 4). In fact, these theorists believe that mass culture was produced by the culture industry as a way of placating the masses, contrary to its democratic appeal, and that its "subliminal message...was/[is] conformity and resignation" (Armaline et al. 1994, 184). The sexism and racism that often plagues punk rock are used as examples of how punk rock serves the interests of dominant society, underscoring the argument that the masses do not have any culture with which they can resist the dominant culture (Giroux & Simon 1989).

Giroux and Simon (1989) argue that theorists from the Frankfurt School, such as Adorno, are too one-sided in their analysis of popular culture and that this perspective on popular culture:

> has little to do with complex and contradictory notions of consent and opposition, which necessitate exploring the pedagogical principles that structure how people negotiate, mediate, affirm, or reject particular aspects of the terrain of the popular. Instead, the popular collapses into an unproblematic sphere of domination where critical thought and action remain a distant memory of the past (p. 5).

There is another more contemporary view of popular culture that Giroux and Simon (1989) argue is just as limiting as the one offered by Adorno, which they refer to as the "culture of authenticity." Those who subscribe to this perspective hold that the logic and practices of the culture industry have no influence on certain subcultures such as punk rock. This romantic view of popular culture holds that certain subcultures and working-class cultures escape the contradictions of the larger society. Giroux and Simon critique this perspective for not acknowledging the complexities of cultural production and reproduction:

> In failing to acknowledge popular culture as one sphere in a complex field of domination and subordination, this view ignores the necessity of providing an understanding of how power produces different levels of cultural relations, experiences, and values that articulate the multi-layered ideologies and social practices of any society (p. 6).

In sum, these perspectives view culture as an artifact, but overlook the multidimensional nature of struggles, contradictions, and re-formations that in different ways characterize the "historically specific surface of popular cultural forms" (p. 7). In response, theories of resistance attempt to revise these theories by describing the ways in which cultural relations both enable and disable individuals in specific social contexts (Giroux & Simon 1989).

According to Armaline et al. (1994), Marx, Gramsci, and the Frankfurt School all held that education played two major roles in reproducing capitalist society: "(1) the preparation of people for varying roles in the labor force; and (2) ideological indoctrination and control" (p. 185). These ideas have been expanded upon and revised by a wide range of radical educational theorists including Aronowitz and Giroux (1985), Dreeben (1968), Jackson (1968), and Simon et al. (1991), among many others. The following is an overview of theories of resistance and postmodernism, which helps us better understand and contextualize the musical phenomenon of punk rock and its role in subverting and accommodating capitalist relations.

Resistance

According to Peter McLaren in *Life in Schools* (1989), schooling in general tends to deemphasize free thought and discourages the empowerment of teachers and students, thus reproducing the "technocratic and corporate ideologies that characterize dominant societies" (p. 1). Public education in general, therefore, contributes to the conditioning of citizens who think and act as the system wishes them to; that is, in the interests of the capitalist system, which is to reproduce the relations of capitalist production. McLaren among others, including Aronowitz and Giroux (1985; 1993) and Shor (1992), take the critique of capitalist education to another level by including the complex and often contradictory ideas of student resistance.

Shor (1992) and Chávez Chávez (1998) focus on the ways in which students reared in an increasingly conservative environment are resisting more and more democratic pedagogical attempts at multicultural education, which is of the utmost importance to understand for those of us working for a more just society as educators. Here we refer to students' attempts at resisting traditional, oppressive education (i.e., the banking method). Such resistance, according to McLaren (1989), is made possible by the partial autonomy of school culture and "the role of conflict and contradiction within the reproductive process itself" (p. 187). In *Pedagogy of the Oppressed*, Paulo Freire (1970b) highlights how education helps to stifle the creativity of students (and teachers) in an effort to condition their consciousnesses with the ideas, values, and beliefs of the dominant (oppressor) culture, which results in what he calls *domestication*. Despite these forces, Freire stresses that creativity, which can be limited, cannot totally be eliminated, for creativity—our ability to humanize the world through culture—is an innate human trait. In other words, despite the fact that our humanity, in this case our ability to create culture, can be limited, it cannot totally be destroyed. Therefore, an understanding of the complexities of culture is needed to understand "the relationship between schools and dominant society" (McLaren 1989, 187).

In *Learning to Labor: How Working Class Kids Get Working Class Jobs*, Paul Willis (1977) highlights what he sees as the self-destructiveness of the culture of working-class boys who resist what he calls "mental labor" at school. They also often engage in sexist and racist activities as "acting out." According to Willis, much of the culture of the working class furthers the interests of the dominant classes and reinforces the roles of the working class as laborers. However, Willis did believe that working-class youth could become revolutionaries, but by resisting mental labor. The school could not help the boys move beyond the factory and shop floor occupations their parents had, but young people can and do rebel against this system, which we find articulated in music. For example, in a hip-hop song entitled "they schools" by the African American group Dead Prez, schools that represent the interests of white, dominant, capitalist society are identified as being of little use to the African American community. For Dead Prez, schools do not teach African American students how to deal with issues central to their lives, like getting crack out of their neighborhoods and creating a strong, self-sufficient community. Dead Prez concludes in "they schools" that "they schools" aren't needed for the revolution.

Noting why many students, especially students of color, reject dominant society's schools, McLaren (1989) observes that: "Students reject the culture of classroom learning because, for the most part, it is delibidinalized and is infused with a cultural capital to which subordinate groups have little legitimate access" (p. 188). Cultural capital, according to McLaren:

> represents ways of talking, acting, modes of style, moving, socializing, forms of knowledge, language practices, and values. Cultural capital can exist in the embodied state, as long-lasting dispositions of the mind and body; in the objectified state, as cultural artifacts such as...books, diplomas...and in the institutionalized state, which confers original properties on the cultural capital which it guarantees (p. 190).

The culture of the dominant group is the culture that is assigned the most institutionalized value. Schools in the United States overtly and covertly look to assimilate all students so that they will embrace the culture of white, middle-class, heterosexual, male values. Schools, therefore, socialize students not to value the culture they bring with them to school. In fact, according to McLaren, those who employ speech patterns of the middle class are more often affirmed and rewarded, while those who employ working-class speech patterns are devalued in school.

Cultural capital thus becomes symbolic of the structure of economic forces and "becomes in itself a productive force in the reproduction of social relations under capitalism" (McLaren 1989, 191). Thus the culture of the dominant group is indeed part of its hegemony, for its values, ideas, and expected social outcomes become normalized and naturalized. Those who do not possess or hold to these values (or those who deviate the most from them) are labeled abnormal and/or deviant. For McLaren, working-class, anticapitalist resistance is an attempt by individuals and communities to maintain some degree of autonomy and individuality. However, being relatively powerless, working-class individuals have little impact on the system in general without an organized movement. A closer look at working-class resistors sheds light on past, present, and potential efforts at organizing for change.

Some scholars (Aronowitz and Giroux 1985; McLaren, 1989) conceptualize student resistors much the same way Gramsci conceptualized organic intellectuals. According to McLaren, student resistors are "intellectuals...who question prevailing norms and established regimes of truth" (p. 189). These resisting intellectuals are largely resisting ignorance, as they argue is perpetuated through U.S. culture by the mass media, schools, and other cultural institutions. Joe Strummer of Clash stressed this anti-ignorance theme prevalent in punk rock in an interview with Mike Flood Page and quoted by Bruce Dancis in

Pins and Class Struggle: Punk Rock and the Left" (1978). "We're anti-fascist, we're anti-violence, we're anti-racist, and we're pro-creative. We're against ignorance" (p. 70). These punk social critics are in direct contradiction with dominant culture (McLaren 1989). It is therefore not surprising that punkers and their music are often targets of state-based repression. For example, Jello Biafra, owner of the Alternative Tentacles punk record label, one-time singer for the Dead Kennedys, and current singer with Lard, was formally accused of "distribution of harmful matter to minors" (Lewis, 1997) in the 1980's-led music censoring by Tipper Gore and others. Because of a hung jury, Biafra et al. were not prosecuted. The case, however, took Biafra's career in a new direction. Following the trial, Biafra went on a speaking tour that resulted in the release of a slew of "spoken word" albums (discussed in Chapter 8, pp. 95-117). Given Jello Biafra's response to the censorship and punk's overall anticapitalist resistance stance, here we ask the question: What role is punk rock to play in U.S. society? To answer the question, we start by briefly outlining the history of punk rock, which we address more in depth in Chapters 3 and 4 (pp. 41--64). We outline the following body of literature and interpret it using the notions of resistance outlined above.

In "The Future Is Unwritten: Working-Class Youth Cultures in England and America," Benj DeMott (1988) argues implicitly that punk rock emerged in England as a musical genre during the 1970s. It emerged as a reaction to the living conditions that existed after World War II and the breakdown of kinship patterns and community ties. Youth subcultures, according to DeMott, served to ease family tension by refocusing it on adults in general. In other words, youth refocused the anger they felt toward the adults they encountered at home on the street and at school, which resulted in youth countercultures. Thus, punk rock emerged as "a generational-specific symbolic system" (p. 42), a white, male, working-class phenomena that provided young men with a way of creating autonomy and difference from their parents and their culture. In addition, DeMott stresses the working-class nature of punk rock as a response to a burgeoning postwar poverty. Still, DeMott's overemphasis on punk rock's anti-adult stance draws attention away from the importance of the class-based element of punk and the influence of larger social structures on it. *The Filth and the Fury: A Sex Pistols Film* (2000), directed by Julien Temple, for example, contextualized the Sex Pistols and punk rock in general as a working-class phenomenon that emerged out of the frustration and anger of England's working class, given conditions in England's postwar economy. And not surprising to some, one pattern in the music culture that emerged, given the patriarchal, heterosexist, racist histories in both the United States and England, was that the punk rockers who received the most notoriety, such as the Sex Pistols, were male, light skinned, and portrayed as heterosexual. Nonetheless, scholars such as Simon Frith (1982), have convincingly interpreted the punk rock that has entered the mainstream as representative of the streets or the underground.

According to Frith, young women have been largely restricted from punk by the gender system in which they live, because most young women, unlike most of their male counterparts, were and are restricted to their homes during adolescence. Frith also notes that parents exert control over young women, more so than young men. Young women were and are restricted from going out and participating in street culture with boys. Young women's restriction to the home is due in part to society's expectation that young girls will grow up to be housewives. As a result, parents and society at large kept and keep young women from participating in the creative negotiations taking place in the streets out of which punk rock emerged. Restrictions engendered by prescribed gender roles have therefore served to severely limit women's active participation in the creation of punk rock. According to Frith, punk rock may have emerged as a form of resistance, but failed to resist the gender roles of dominant society. Yet despite these gender expectations, Frith and others failed to recognize the breadth of punk audiences. In *The Filth and the Fury* (2000), much of the film footage of some of the first punk rock shows (in England) contained just as many women as men in the crowd. This suggests that maybe the male dominance of punk rock is more a result of the mainstream music industry, which signed some of the first punk bands before the emergence of underground, independent labels. That is to say, the selection by music promoters may be giving us a false perception that punk culture reproduced society's gender norms. According to Cohen (1972), quoted in DeMott (1988), the unstated function of countercultures such as punk is to "express and negotiate 'contradictions which were hidden or unresolved in the parent culture'" (p. 42), which can help us understand the presence, however invisible, of women in punk rock. It also could be argued that working-class women's oppressive relations to their male counterparts created the anger and frustration in them that resulted in a strong base of female punkers, which we address later in this book. But we can say, in sum, that England's punk rock scene emerged as a result of unmaterialized promises of economic rewards.

We note, however, that according to Bruce Dancis (1978) and Richard Dixon et al. (1979) that there are clear distinctions between British punk and

U.S. punk. These distinctions are important because there are scholars who write as if punk was one category, which we and others (Dancis 1978) see as problematic.

> British punk often concerns working-class themes, particularly youthful unemployment and the lack of opportunity that come out of the life experiences of the musicians. In the United States punk rock has little of this class dimension, and the social protest it does contain often seems postured (Dancis 1978, 63).

Dixon et al. (1979) makes a similar, yet less delineated distinction between British and U.S. punk. "The lyrics are typically an angry and political railing against the ills of established society" (although U.S. punk rock groups are more focused on sex, violence, drugs, death, and violations of etiquette) (p. 211). According to Lewis (1997), however, around the beginning of the 1980s there was a shift in the emergence of more critical punkers from the United Kingdom to the United States.

> [T]he inept bumbling offered by most of the UK's punk bands at this time could not compare [to the Dead Kennedys]. In fact, the focus of articulation and intelligent hardcore was switching to the U.S...and to this day the U.S. has remained its most fertile breeding ground (p. 4).

Traditionally the punk rock at the forefront of the punk scene served to bring attention to white, male-centered economic social injustices through both music and style of dress articulating punk conceptions of masculinity and male working-class culture.

However, punk rock was not exclusive to straight white men. People of African descent, Latinas/os, white women, lesbian women of various ethnic racial groups, and gay men have all appealed to the punk rock aesthetic, largely as a reaction to both the dominant punk aesthetic and the ideas, values, and beliefs of dominant societies. The Tom Robinson Band, the Jam, and The Gang of Four are examples of British punk bands that identify with and are supported by gay communities (Dancis 1978). And the queer punk scene in the United States is represented by an articulation of difference and identity (Fenster 1992), which became a phenomenon in the 1980s. Fenster notes that:

> B]oth the local scenes and national institutions of punk and hardcore music, which have an audience and musician-base of middle- and lower-middle class white teenagers and post-adolescents, were articulated almost exclusively to a notion of the music as

> performed for and by heterosexuals....Queer punks describe themselves as feeling forced to stifle expression of their sexual preference in these sites for fear of both physical assault...and the more generalized and symbolic violence of homophobia....Recently, however, the issue of homosexuality has been confronted in punk and hardcore sites on a number of fronts: in bands, [and] in particular scenes (most notably in San Francisco)...(p. 135).

According to Fenster, the rise of the queer punk scene is not only a response to the homophobia prevalent in punk, but also reflects dimensions of "conservative political backlashes against previous and current gains in homosexual civil rights, and the political and cultural conservatism of some middle-class assimilationist homosexuals" (p. 155). In addition, access to punk rock is important for many homosexuals because of punk's general rejection of "'disco-consumptive' aspects of dominant gay culture" (p. 157). Furthermore, the emergence of the queer punk scene made "possible a set of identities for those gays and lesbians who have tastes for and who participate in cultural practices which are tied more closely to hardcore and punk" (p. 157). Therefore, punk can serve to subvert not only dominant society but also punk itself. The following is an overview of other dimensions of punk music.

The Clash, an early English punk band, embodies the traditional punk aesthetic. The predominant message of their music is that of working-class protest against youth unemployment, poverty, authoritarianism, racism, and fascism. The Clash's music, and punk rock in general, is "an authentic, unfiltered expression of the fears, anxiety, sexual needs, and anger that rumble down the corridors of high schools, colleges, factories, and offices" (Dancis 1978, 62). Contrary to the views of such scholars as London (1984), who claimed that U.S. punk rock "doesn't have the following necessary to sustain itself" (p. 167), a number of scholars hold that punk rock is not a passing trend or a fad with a rope (Dancis 1978; Morthland 1985; McDonald 1987; Epstein 1994). It is true that until recently U.S. punk has not had widespread appeal due to the very nature of punk rock, but punk rock in the United States exists underground and thus invisible in its pure form on MTV and is rarely heard on the radio (Davies 1994). It is virtually impossible for a punk band to enter the mainstream and remain punk, for punk is antiestablishment. Bands like Rancid, Bad Religion, and Green Day emerged in the underground as punk rockers, but it can be argued that once they entered the mainstream they lost many of their community ties largely due to the distancing created by their shows, unaffordable for most punkers of working-class backgrounds. One might argue that their music has become a watered-down commodification of "turning rebellion into money" (Davies 1994, 4). One might also argue that examples of punk rock mainstream success might be instances of victory, that is, spreading the message to a wider audience (given the message is still emancipatory in nature). Johny Rotten of the Sex Pistols in *The Filth and the Fury* (2000) argued that mainstream success has had a negative effect on the punk movement because it changed the meaning of the punk style by making it acceptable, thus sucking it back up into what Rotten calls the "shitstem" (system). No doubt, this is not an easy call, and it is clear how someone (an academic, for example) who is not or has never been part of the punk scene might think it is doomed. Punk is a form of grass-roots resistance, and because of corporate intervention, as noted above, it will most likely not grow into a large movement but also will probably not fade away because angry youths are always with us (Dancis 1978). "Stiff Little Fingers noted on their second album release, on Side A "PUNK IS DEAD, BUT..." and then on the other side read "WE'RE STILL DYING" (Davies 1994, 17). According to Davies (1994) "real punks" are not the stars who were once punk but "the unknowns and the underground who sustain a politically active and subversive tendency to this day" (p. 4).

It is the ever-growing impact of the globalization of capitalism that makes us certain that the existence of angry youth will not fade away any time soon, as many punkers and rappers point out in recent songs. Things are fucked up, they say; the revolution is and will not be pretty, and things will only get worse before they get better. One of the most common locations for social inequality and anomie is in schools across the United States. Violence in the schools today by angry and dislocated youth is proving fertile ground for the views expressed in punk rock. Thus, punk rock in the United States and Britain, despite their differences, tends to view the education system as oppressive and disempowering and thus rejects it. Note the following series suggested in lyrics by U.S. punk:

> Mommy's little monster dropped out of school...
> He doesn't want to be a doctor or a lawyer get fat and rich...

These lines were excerpted from Social Distortion's song "Mommy's Little Monster" on *Time Bomb* records, and published in 1983.

> Carter power will soon go away
> I will be Fuher one day
> I will command all of you

> Your kids will mediate in school…

This excerpt is from the Dead Kennedys' song "California Über Alles" on *Alternative Tentacles*, and published in 1980.

> So you been to school
> for a year or two
> and you know you've seen it all…

Another excerpt from the Dead Kennedys, these lines were taken from the song "Holiday in Cambodia," from the record *Fresh Fruit for Rotting Vegetables*, reprinted with permission courtesy of Decay Music 1980.

> Are you trying to say that I'm crazy, well I went to your schools, I went to your churches, I went to your institutional learning facilities, so how can you say I'm crazy? I'm not crazy, institution. You're the one who's crazy, institution…

Finally, these lyrics were taken from the Suicidal Tendencies' song "Institutionalized" on *Frontier Records*, and published in 1983.

And from British punk, we note from the song "Fall Out" by the Police: "I said my education it was my indoctrination just to be another cog in a machine" (Dancis 1978, 69). By no means are the songs quoted above representative of all of punk rock in either the United States or Britain, but a number of music scholars do suggest that punk rock is a form of anticapitalist resistance. Part of that resistance includes resistance to the ideological indoctrination of schools (McDonald 1987; Morthland 1985; Dancis 1978).

Other punk scholars disagree and suggest that punk rock in many ways serves to reproduce ideologies of dominant, capitalist societies. As demonstrated by Willis in his ethnography *Learning to Labor* (1977), youth resistance is not always solely about resisting dominant, capitalist society. Quite often, youth resistance results in the perpetuation of established class structures and ideological hierarchies, of which punk rock is often guilty. Much of punk rock assists in the reproduction of patriarchal as well as homophobic ideologies. Like in rock and roll, there has been a misogynistic side to punk from its inception in both Britain and the United States, expressed by New York City–based bands like the Velvet Underground and the New York Dolls, the San Francisco–based Avengers, and the British-based Cortinas (Dancis 1978). Male punk rockers have often expressed more explicit hostility and violence toward women than popular rock and roll. Bands such as the Dead Boys and ıbody misogyny expressed all too often in their lyrics. In Fear's *More Bear*, the song "Strangulation" is a disturbing example of punk y:

Gonna strangle me a bitch
Gonna leave her in a ditch...
I'm gonna chop off her tits...
Gonna mess with her head
Gonna tie her to the bed
Strangulation
Mutilation
Humiliation...

This punk rock song represents a self-destructiveness that supports using women, particularly poor women of color, as objects of exploitation.

Songs such as these serve the interests of dominant groups because they attack two groups that could be potential allies. Working women are portrayed as inferior to working men and promoted as objects to be used by working men to abuse, subordinate, and dominate, rather than as humans to be in struggle with and against an exploitative economic system. Similar to rock and roll, in punk the number of women musicians to defend themselves are few. When women do enter the punk scene, it is usually as sex objects or even objects for physical abuse (Dancis 1978).

Women have been largely excluded from this musical genre. The status of women in this counterculture has traditionally not been unlike that in other popular music venues, often subject to sexual violence. When women do enter the punk counterculture as performers, they frequently must employ the traditional male aesthetic in order to be taken seriously because of the male dominance and masculine norms of the record industry. This male-centered dominant ideology is at times expressed as racism.

Punk bands that are known as racists such as Screwdriver, a white power skinhead band, utilize punk to portray racist and fascist messages. The Nuns, a punk band with a woman lead singer, not known as a racist band, did produce the following racist song.

I own all the projects
on 101st Avenue
I hate the niggers
And the Puerto Ricans too

> Cause I'm a decadent Jew...
>
> Excerpt from The Nuns, "Decadent Jew," 415 Records 1978.

This racist use of punk rock represents another way working people are encouraged to be divided instead of uniting around their marginal status as workers. Because this song portrays Jews in the United States as racists and greedy, and because The Nuns do not have a reputation as racists, this song could be read as potentially more influential, dangerous, and beneficial to dominant group interest. It is this extreme nature of the punk aesthetic that makes it a useful tool for not only radical leftists, but also for extreme conservative right-wingers, such as Fear.

Applying resistance theory critique, punk rock serves both to produce and reproduce capitalist interests. On the one hand it promotes a sexism and racism that goes against the potential for like-status individuals to mobilize politically. On the other hand, punk resists class-based exploitation and oppression by going against the ideological indoctrination of capitalist interests in schools that too often also contributes to dividing like-status individuals by covertly and overtly promoting patriarchal and racist ideologies. Thus, punk rock both resists and accommodates dominant society in both the United States and Britain (and other countries where punk is popular) through the multidimensional nature of struggles, contradictions, and reformations (Giroux & Simon 1989).

A related question not addressed thus far is: How do punkers themselves articulate the meaning and purpose of their own counterculture, punk rock, in relation to that of the dominant capitalist culture? We address the question through an analysis of the experiences and perceptions of one of the authors of this book—Curry Malott. In this next section, he speaks from personal experience.

As stated earlier, I came of age in Oregon during the 1980s as a skater/punk, and punk rock has been a central part of my life ever since; even when I was not participating, punk ideals were still present. In retrospect, punk music and skateboarding, together, were a way of life for me, and many of my close friends and allies throughout the West Coast (see Chapter 4 for more on the relationship between skateboarding and punk rock, pp. 61-64). Skateboarding and punk rock were not just things we did and consumed. We lived them as creators and perpetuators of punk. We were punks and lived our lives throughout the Reagan/Bush years accordingly. In other words, our experiences were and are impacted by the social context in which we were and are all embedded, because none of us live in isolation from the world around us.

What follows is my own perception of some of the values and norms we in skaterpunk counterculture held, and our perceptions of some of the values and norms held by what we perceived as the dominant culture. Although we were aware of the fact that we lived in a capitalist society, we did not always refer to it as such. In the discussion that follows, Milagros Peña and I will therefore not refer to U.S. society as a capitalist-based culture, but just as the dominant culture. It is helpful to think of the following values and norms of the dominant culture and my own specific punk rock counterculture as on a continuum where the dominant side represents the far right or conservative side, and the punk side represents the far left or the radical side. Milagros and I are not arguing that punk is inherently Left and mainstream or inherently Right; this was just a perception of the world. As we will argue, the lives of most punkers were not totally radical or conservative, nor totally resistive or accommodative, but constantly being negotiated in complex and contradictory ways that coincide with ideas of resistance.

The first of the values to be discussed—material possessions—varied widely on the continuum for the skaters that I (Curry Malott) shared most of my experiences with. I thought that proponents of the dominant culture highly valued material possessions and we frowned upon them for being materialistic and valuing private property more than human lives. Many of my friends, including myself, however, did not think it was problematic or contradictory to place much importance and value on our cars, skateboards, guitars, and so forth. However, there were some skaters I knew who were radical on this point. Skaterpunkhippies would not even ride in a car, much less own one, because by supporting the automobile industry they were supporting capitalist hegemony and dominant society and, more importantly, contributing to the destruction of the earth. A simple and limited argument, but nonetheless an attempt to connect thought and action.

Not only the destruction of the earth, but the destruction of the body and mind by excessively using alcohol and cocaine, we believed to be common among those individuals on the dominant side of the continuum like most of our teachers and parents. Alcohol and cocaine were therefore associated with over consumption and loss of control, which, in part, stemmed from some of our parents' and siblings' excessive usage. Still, we also valued drug use, but only drugs that we believed to be beneficial and not physically addictive. Marijuana was and is very common among the skaterpunk community on the West Coast. We believed that marijuana enabled us to achieve a more critical perspective of the world as well as improve our skating and music-making abilities. We often used the term "wits" to refer to marijuana because we believed that when under its influence, individuals could be more witty, to have your wits about you. Our positive conception of marijuana was in direct contradiction to dominant society's portrayal of the dumb, loser, burned-out stoner often seen on TV. We also believed that LSD and psychedelic mushrooms or "shrooms" as we called them took our consciousness to higher levels. We used LSD quite often, as frequently as a couple of times a week. LSD was often referred to as "skate medicine" because we also believed it improved our ability to skate as well as critically think and make music, not just play music already recorded. We believed that we could achieve positive effects from these drugs because it would raise our consciousness.

We thought that individuals on the dominant side of the continuum possessed a consciousness that resulted in negative effects when using any consciousness-altering substance. In other words, we believed that those on the dominant side were negative and that no drug could change that, only enhance it. Of course there were contradictions within our counterculture. For example, some drank excessively, but those people tended to be the "old schoolers," the ones who had been around for a long time and were usually written off as old, crazy, and had already paid their dues. Heavy drinking and drug use, heroine ("crank") in particular, also tended to be common among less dedicated skaters, non musicians, and the generally non-focused and less fortunate. Some punkers I knew were born into hard drug biker cultures, which in our counterculture, made their involvement with drugs most of us wouldn't even consider using understandable. There were therefore numerous contradictions and exceptions to our general rules, but there was never any doubt who *we* were and who *they* were, which brings me to the next three values in my punk culture.

We did not value high school at all because we saw it as too controlling, restrictive, and *they*—high school teachers, administrators, etc.—taught us lies. Many of us, on the other hand, accepted dominant society's notion that college is valuable and a way to achieve vertical social mobility, though it is hard to go to college without finishing high school and so rarely pursued. Obviously, we believed that the dominant society highly valued both high school and college education. We also valued employability, but not in the conventional sense as indicated by our attitudes toward education. We valued the status of professional skaters and punk rockers. These professions (ways of life) did not and do not generate much income, which coincided with our conceptions of those with lots of money as greedy, and we frowned upon them. A few professional skaters during the 1980s achieved financial success, but they and the companies they represented were for the most part boycotted as part of the status quo (*them*). Prestige, not money, was the valued fruit these occupations bore, which to us made it more than worthwhile. Our community was our family—for some their only family—and what our peers thought of us meant the world to us. To be respected all along the West Coast by other skaterpunks for your skating or punk music was the ultimate dream. This idealized individuality was a source of contradiction. We supposedly valued our community more than our selves, yet our biggest dreams situated ourselves as individual superstars. So how did we control such blatant individuality almost in direct contradiction to community relationships, namely those within the working classes and those between workers across race and gender?

Unlike a dominant culture that relies on a violent and repressive army state for social control, which we were often subjected to, we relied on each other for social control. We tried to keep each other in line when we crossed our own socially constructed boundaries. For example, the extreme environmentalists of the group made sure to remind the rest of us how much destruction we were doing to the planet by driving our cars, building our wooden ramps, plugging in our high-power guitar amps, and so forth. We kept each other from getting involved in debilitating drugs like cocaine or "crank" by peer pressure. We also tried to eliminate racism, and to a lesser extent sexism, by employing similar tactics. We reduced the racism we were able to detect by simply calling each other on statements or actions viewed as racist. Once someone was called on racism, that person was shunned for an amount of time consistent with both the magnitude and context of the offense.

Subtle racist ideas of white-skinned superiority are such a central component of U.S. society and individual identities (Tatum 1997), it is often hard to detect. As a result most people, including the counterculture I was a part of, do not think of themselves as racist, although the very act of thinking of oneself as morally superior is a result of white supremacy indoctrination. It was dominant society, however, that we saw as the racist ones and we tied them to Reagan's racist politics, which dominated the 1980s (i.e., taxing the poorest of the poor), as well as what high school teachers taught us about American colonialism (i.e., Columbus as a hero). Sexism, on the other hand, was much more accepted and thus blatant and rampant with me and among my male peers. We checked each other occasionally for blatant sexism like telling a woman she couldn't skate or play punk music because of her sex. We rarely checked more subtle forms of sexism, forms too ingrained in our own consciousness. Sexism related to acts of sex and boy/girl relationships were the most frequent. It was usually only in the presence of women skaterpunks that the issue of sexism came up in conversation. I don't remember us ever deeming homophobia as a form of sexism as problematic. In fact, a common occurrence was to call someone "homo" or "butt-pirate," which meant homosexual. In this respect our counterculture served to support dominant society's marginalization of those who are deemed homosexual, see themselves as homosexual, or who have chosen to practice non-heterosexual forms of sexuality.

The last two norms that we saw as differentiating us from the rest of mainstream society were in our appearance and style of music. We saw the dominant cultural norm for appearance and musical style as polished, homogeneous, and essentially processed. In contrast we saw ourselves as original works of art, where no two of us looked the same. Similarly, we saw our music as unpolished, original, and characterized by a hectic, fuck-you attitude. We failed to see how the boundaries we set for ourselves also served to create homogeneity. We also failed to see how the punk aesthetic was being manipulated to fit many disparate political orientations, which brings Milagros and me to a discussion of postmodern perspectives and punk.

Postmodernism

For both of us, trained in the social sciences, postmodernist critiques of positivism helped us critique our methods of analysis and discussion of punkers and punk rock. As sociologists we were trained to distance ourselves from our subjects and the manner in which we write when we speak about them. Consequently, we are more aware of our own internalized values and beliefs and their impact on knowledge production and scientific knowledge in particular. The work of Pauline Marie Rosenau (1992) places emphasis on the way our analytical lenses are filtered through the world we experience and how that informs what we see and interpret. Even the tendency to speak in the passive voice or the use of the third person in academic writing to relate observation creates a comfortable false sense that objective analysis has taken place. Postmodernist critiques on questions of objectivity freed us to do this work together, sometimes with one of our own voices and other times with both. We were careful to allow our own perspectives to come through, and not speak for each other, particularly when our individual experiences were important to emphasize a point and to give voice to experiences we had as individuals. We reject buying into the discourse of scientism (Freire 1998). The modernist claims scientific objectivity and neutrality in her or his scholarship assuming that truth can only be known through an unbiased lens. Such claims serve to mask the class-, race-, and sex-based interests of modern science from those impacted by the isms, as well as from the ones claiming objectivity.

The scientist, through his or her scientific training and conditioning, and simply by living in society, is deceived just as he or she deceives through reproducing that which was ingrained in him or her. In our view, the academy reproduces hegemony and serves to transmit the values and ideas of the dominant classes and overtly and covertly supports, as normal and natural, claims it makes in an unquestioned manner. Instead, we recognize that like society at large, the dominant culture of the university is white, male, upper and middle class. At most universities, white, male, middle-and upper-class discourse is the norm and considered the superior discourse in real science. We argue that when the voice of the academic is passive or hidden, so too is the classism, racism, and sexism, and when presented via a scientific method is to be unquestioned.

As a result, even progressive academics who denounce racism, sexism, and classism, unconsciously position themselves as experts using voices of authority and thus forget the myriad ways in which they too internalize their superiority in whiteness, gender, and class. Raising this issue of voice—who has it, who asserts it, and how—is done here to be critical of our own approach to looking at punk and punk culture, in which we did appeal to scientific methods in our research. We simply want to affirm that the discussion thus far and the analysis that will follow assume the biases we bring to our analysis of punk rock. This critical awareness is important to note. Assuming a critical stance challenges us and other writers to push further on critical thought with the expectation that to learn requires acting on the learning (Wink 2000; Shor 1992; Freire 1998). For us, an active critical voice is what Freire (1998) identified as the foundation for critical consciousness and social action.

While the postmodernist critique of science and research encompasses a wide variety of theoretical perspectives, many stem from a rejection of an enlightenment-based approach to producing grand narratives—that is, a fixed, static, predetermined epistemology. We respond to the critique here by giving punk a sense of agency, allowing punkers to speak for themselves through their music and interviews. It is a way of articulating dimensions of punk resistance, but there are critics to this assertion.

Philip Corrigan (1989) suggests that punk rock is not a form of working-class resistance, nor do those who perform this musical genre have the potential to become organic intellectuals, for these are mere "re-presentations" of the "Other." In other words, to label punk rockers as organic intellectuals is to categorize them as one particular thing thus distorting the complex nature of society. Corrigan argues that whenever an observer attempts to re-present the observed, the result is always surreal. In this view, we cannot categorize social phenomena into limiting categories without distorting the complexity of society, and we cannot describe social phenomena without imposing our own biases on our descriptions. Jude Davies (1994) takes this dedifferentiation approach a step further than Corrigan. Davies does not differentiate between punk rock and popular rock. In Davies' work, punk rock is not treated as a subculture in opposition with dominant popular culture. Davies rejects the notion that punk's political significance lies in its resistance to dominant culture. Davies instead focuses on the subversiveness of punk within dominant culture. In other words, through *dissensus* punk rock created and continues to create a space for social discourse excluded by society's expectations in giving in to consensus and conformity.

For punks, communication and politics are problematic because they are grounded in a notion of consensus that serves to silence a minority or those who are outsiders by society's norms. Outsiders, constructed as others, are framed by discourse that secures the reproduction of the status quo. Punk rock in these terms can be viewed as postmodern because it serves to deconstruct consensus. In doing so, punkers have successfully rejected "some of the dictates and operation of the dominant culture" (Marx & McAdam 1994, 19) by creating their own record labels and fanzines[1], thus empowering themselves to be heard in their own socially constructed space. Punk rock is part of the dissensus that one could argue was present in the spirit of earlier rock music. It is part of a popular culture that stands as a challenge to society's status quo.

As such, punk rock as a postmodern musical genre resists society from within popular culture. To unravel what some may argue are seemingly theoretical contradictions, we apply Rosenau's (1992) framework for understanding the various positions in postmodernist theory. We argue that punk rock can be articulated at times as a form of negative or skeptical postmodernism, while at other times it takes the form of positive or affirmative postmodernism. The former asserts that there is nothing salvageable in society, so let's destroy it. The latter recognizes some aspects of society as good, but looks to salvage the good with healthy skepticism. The difference between positive and negative postmodern punk is not always easily identified. Sometimes bands change their positions from song to song or more commonly from album to album.

Some punk rockers, like post–Sex Pistols Johny Rotten on their single *World Destruction* with Africa Bambaataa, believe that society is in a perpetual state of decay and that we are doomed for destruction and are thus characterized by defeatism and nihilism. They subscribe to an apolitical stance because struggle is meaningless and individuals are powerless to effect change due to the corruption of government and politicians on both the Left and the Right. The skeptics therefore see nonpolitical participation as a healthy protest to representative democracy. Furthermore, the skeptics argue that political engagement has led to slaughter, repression, and genocide in the name of nationalism and patriotism. These postmodern skeptics hold that the best we can do is to be passionately passive (Rosenau 1992).

Rather than invest in movements for social change, many of what we can call negative postmodern punkers are preoccupied with death and destruction. Terrorism, violence, and protest become anti conventional postmodern forms of nonrepresentational political participation. These forms of political participation contradict modern conceptions of the "normal" and are in fact contemptuous of it (Rosenau 1992). Violence thus becomes an anti-text, where events create structure and structure creates events (Rosenau 1992). For example, suicide, for the most extreme skeptics, has become "the only authentic political gesture left, the last and most revolutionary act, the culmination of post-modern resistance" (p. 143). Thus, in *The Filth and the Fury* (2000), former Sex Pistol, John Lyden, described the group as self-destructing from their very beginning and stated that they didn't last because they were real—only the fakes last. Their demise was a revolutionary act because they refused to be a cog in the capitalist society and music industry machine. Through self-destructing you take with you as much of the system as possible.

On the flipside, positive postmodern punkers take the critique of the modern idea of progress and use it to create a better world for everyone. While these, what we may call affirmative postmodern punkers, also won't participate in traditional institutionalized political movements that have totalizing ideologies (one fixed reality) and an identified end goal (replacing capitalism with socialism), they do not believe in dismantling one hierarchical system only to replace it with another. They question prescribed and officially accepted forms of gaining knowledge (schooling), paper qualifications (credentials), and notions of expertise or experts, and so forth.

These types of positive postmodernists are more optimistic and believe that a progressive postmodern epistemology and ontology can be used in the interests of democracy and thus for social change by acknowledging that reality is a result of human experience and knowledge is created out of those experiences. As people reflect on their own experiences, situating them in broader, social, historical contexts, they can and do democratically create new actions and experiences in struggle together that are relevant to their own lives. Such a perspective has the potential to bring all working- and middle-class people together because by critically reflecting on our own experiences, we realize the source of our problems, although materialized in different ways. There is the recognition that our conceptions of reality are historically based and culturally influenced, but constantly changing because of the new potentials created in social movements, which create potential for new alliances among different social groups. For example, new political movements born out of feminism and green politics encourage this perspective.

In progressive postmodernism everyone has and is given a voice. By this view, promoting what progressive postmodern punkers believe will result in the inclusion of all kinds of people and thus a healthy, democratic dissensus—meaning we can respect that we do not all have to be together on all issues to coexist. As such, not all punkers are antipolitical, but do criticize those who participate in representative democracy for legitimating the state. This second type of punkers, what we call, using Rosenau's (1992) framework, positive postmodernists, subscribe to grass-roots movements where everyone involved has an equal say in social movement actions and share in equal power. They are activists in de-centered and unorganized protest where members of the movement are not expected to stay long, and leaders are hard to identify, if there are any.

Still, for Philip Corrigan (1989), punk rock as a postmodern musical genre emerged out of what he terms the "pedagogy of governance," which is characterized by a patriarchal paternalism. This patriarchal paternalism coupled with a decaying capitalist world system is what fuels the punk rock postmodern stance as noted by such groups as the Clash and the Sex Pistols. Instead, we note that the Clash, a punk band from Britain, has transcended national boundaries, and classifying bands by country distorts the complex nature of society and thus the way we label them. The Clash are resisting iconoclasts, but are often positive and support the concept of emancipation through both their songs and their involvement with Rock Against Racism. In our view, the Clash can be viewed as supportive of grass-roots political movements where participants have equal voice. These aforementioned political messages are found on some of their last albums.

It is true that the Clash demonstrated their negative cynicism and nihilism in many of their early songs. They attacked their record company, CBS, in their 1978 release "Complete Control." They criticized CBS for not allowing them the artistic freedom they were promised. In "Complete Control," as in many others, they deconstruct popular culture from within. The Clash were fascinated with apocalypse themes as demonstrated on their 1979 releases "London Calling" and "Armagideon Time," a cover version of a reggae classic. These songs are not warnings or celebrations, but they convey an uneasiness that makes the option of giving up out of the question (Davies 1994). The "Clash" utilized a wide variety of musical styles that resisted fixed rules on what was possible in music (Davies 1994).

By contrast, the Sex Pistols typify the apocalypticism of punk (Davies 1994). The Sex Pistols seemingly took William S. Burrough's advice to youth to "take the place apart before the whole planet goes up in flames" (p. 12). Their lyrics "reflect, threaten and sometimes celebrate the disintegration and destruction of society" (p. 12). Their best songs describe a state of alienation and boredom where the inevitable apocalypse seems attractive (Davies 1994). In their song "God Save the Queen" they suggest that the only future is to become an agent of apocalyptic destruction (Davies 1994).

> God Save the Queen
> The fascist regime
> Made you a moron
> Potential H-bomb

Here the Sex Pistols are suggesting that the way to escape a meaningless existence is to become a part of and identify with apocalyptic events (Davies 1994).

Sex Pistols' punk represents a withdrawal from political participation coupled with a sense of desperation and defeatism because punkers are aware that individuals are powerless to change government and society—what Rosenau (1992) describes as a central theme among negative postmodernists. Here, we simply highlight Rosenau's distinction of both positive and negative postmodernism approaches to highlight punkers' rejection of modern institutions, but at the same time to argue that not all punk has to be viewed as nihilistic and negative. We have highlighted, for example, their rejection of schools. But we also want to note that punk represents a wide variety of worldviews—heterosexual, homosexual, working class, middle class, multiracial, and ethnic to name a few. In that way, we can say punk is pluralistic. As such, punk can therefore be read as a postmodern musical genre that is "so abstract and obscurantist that it can be manipulated to fit any political orientation" and in that sense can be claimed by a postmodern stance (p. 166). For those reasons, some ask, is this postmodern position in punk inherently Left wing or Right wing? We answer by assuming Rosenau's position. Rosenau has made a case for postmodernism as neither inherently Left wing nor Right wing. Those who have criticized postmodernism as inherently Right wing have tended to only look at the skeptics, as if they all represented postmodernism (Rosenau 1992). The same can be said for those who argue that postmodernism is inherently radical. We argue that punk is more complex and difficult to describe as inherently either Right wing or Left wing.

Summary

The theoretical perspective informing this study is one that draws on Marxism, neo-Marxism, and progressive postmodernism. Marx's critique of capitalism is of utmost importance and relevant in today's global society (discussed in Chapter 5, pp. 65-68). We have therefore decided to take an overtly class-based approach to our discussion. Consequently, Gramsci's notion of hegemony and the organic intellectual is central to our analysis of why we consent to the capitalist order, and to racism, sexism, and wage labor for example. Finally, a progressive postmodern approach helps us understand the importance of embracing a global society marked by multiple perspectives, realities, and to ultimately adopt multiple approaches for working toward a more democratic, just world. In short, our approach helps us make connections between all of our oppressions, connecting them to common experiences rooted in societies marked by exploitation and alienation. In large part, we are guilty because we consent to participate when we internalize its values, ideas, and beliefs as normal and natural and do not question their effect on us. Finally, the critical awareness that results from this analysis, for us, is largely where the hope for a new, more democratically just society lies. The critical awareness that we speak of results in embracing all of our differences as representative of the human condition—that is, as creative cultural producers—in order to build alliances and new social movements that transcend borders, however we define them. Despite the seeming differences in punk rock messages, punk rock sits squarely among those new social movements that look for ways to build bridges among potential political allies against common enemies—capitalism, fascism, racism, and sexism to name a few. And like so many other movements, punk rock is a product of the social criticisms of its time.

Chapter 3
His-story of Selected Subversive Popular Musical Genres

[1]What follows is a brief overview of the history of some of the subversive musical forms that preceded and influenced some of the first, mostly white, punk rockers in the United States. Punk rock is often credited as coming from white communities, despite the fact that much of the history is rooted in the subversive music of folk and rock and roll singers that emerged out of African American communities. Because of this misperception, we provide a brief history of punk cast in this broader context. From that historical analysis, we outline some of the major studies done on alternative music most relevant to this study's focus on punk's critique of society, particularly critiques of accommodation versus resistance. This history takes us on a journey through some of the deeper meanings of punk rock.

An Historical Perspective

Throughout the history of western civilization political leaders and political activists have recognized the power of music as a force that could potentially affect political ends. The Greek philosopher Plato, in *The Republic*, twenty-three hundred years ago, stated:

> [A]ny musical innovation is full of danger to the whole state, and ought to be prohibited [because it] imperceptibly penetrates into manners and customs; whence issuing with greater force, it invades contracts between man [*sic*, meant to say among people] and man…goes on to laws and constitutions, in utter recklessness, ending at last…by an overthrow of all rights, private as well as public (1928, Book IV, 146).

Consequently, Greek political officials frequently banned music and other forms of expression that posed a threat, either real or imagined, to dominant ideas, values, and beliefs.

Similarly, English monarchs like Henry VIII, Mary I, and Elizabeth I made special points to control ballads and broadsides. Mary I outlawed the distribution of books, ballads, rhymes, and interludes. According to Justice Potter Stewart (1965) quoted by Mumia Abu-Jamal in *All Things Censored* (2000), "censorship reflects a society's lack of confidence in itself. It is a hallmark of an authoritarian regime" (p. 50). No doubt, a government based on injustice can be nothing but paranoid and afraid of the citizens toward which it acts unjustly. An English political writer of the eighteenth century, Andrew Fletcher, expressed the power of songs in the following quote: "give me the making of the songs of a nation, and I care not who makes the laws" (Denisoff 1971, 1). The belief that music can mobilize a nation's people to challenge society's laws and norms traveled with Europeans to the United States.

In the United States sentiments about music's subversive as well as pacifying qualities were shared by those in positions of power—primarily politicians—but also by musicians and political activists. Franklin Roosevelt, during the Depression, was quoted as saying: "If you can sing a song that would make people forget their troubles…I'll give you a medal" (Denisoff 1971, 1). During the 1960s the musical group Peter, Paul, and Mary, realizing the revolutionary potential of music grounded in people's protests, proclaimed:

> Do you realize the power of PP and M? We could mobilize the youth of America today in a way that nobody else could. We could conceivably travel with a presidential candidate, and maybe even sway an election (p. 2).

Peter, Paul, and Mary, like many politicians and musicians in general, realized the mobilizing power of music, which we argue, can manifest itself in complex and contradictory ways, used in commercials as jingles or sung at political demonstrations denouncing the status quo.

As far back as the 1920s many white working people and middle-class radicals drew on and benefited from the revolutionary underpinnings of African American musical traditions and subscribed to the idea that music could be employed as a tool to fight against injustices—at the time fascism. Such messages are inscribed on Woody Guthrie's guitar ("This Machine Kills Fascists") and on Pete Seeger's banjo ("This Machine Surrounds Hate and Forces It to Surrender"). At the time, some claimed that folk singers and rock and roll artists were plotting to "hypnotize and subvert the youth of America" (Denisoff 1971, 2). These examples serve to show how scared people were of the critical consciousness raised by music, particularly the revolutionary call suggested in the lyrics. Thus, folk music and rock and roll have no doubt been created by and for individuals and communities with particular political interests often contrary to those of the ruling class. Consequently, these musical genres and others like them (i.e., punk rock) are therefore liberating and potentially revolutionary on a macro, societal level.

The notion that music can be used as a tool to generate working-class consciousness is not new. It permeates Marxist movements. Lenin, for example, held that art and music should play an integral role in generating agitating propaganda that would "facilitate political consciousness" (Denisoff 1971, 2) among the exploited Russian peasants. Art and music would therefore come to play an important role in revolutionary change throughout the world. In the United States during the 1930s, art, literature, drama, and music were used to unite workers when the "Marxian millennium was believed to be close at hand" (Denisoff 1971, 2). It was the folk music of the American Communist Party that expressed the injustices of capitalism and a cry for change. The music, which largely employed guitars and banjos, was fairly simple so as not to detract from the lyrical messages. The focus of the music was ideal for propaganda purposes, thriving first in rural areas of the southern United States.

Folk music in the United States in its early years, however, was often also conservative and "rarely offered solutions [to social ills that amounted to more than] a good woman, a bottle on Saturday night, or going to heaven" (Denisoff 1971, 15). However, as employment opportunities and conditions became more exploitative in the South, folk songs became more centered in economics and politics. The Highlander folk school and its cofounder, Myles Horton, played a central role in empowering poor whites in the 1920s and 1930s, and African Americans in the 1950s and 1960s, resulting in these groups organizing themselves politically and writing powerful influential folk songs (Horton & Freire 1996). Horton, and Highlander in general, used question-based pedagogy, and a student experience–centered curriculum, for their adult education program designed to challenge adults to critically reflect on their experiences with their fellow workers. The teaching method was designed to help them find solutions to their problems in dialogue with each other, with the idea that the teaching process would produce critically conscious, self-empowered workers as they sought to transform their own realities. Though much of the language, vision, and ideas of Highlander came from academics such as Horton, who was educated at northern universities, his background was that of a poor white Southerner. Yet despite the fact that the Highlander school was shaped by radical hillbillies, other poor and progressive whites, African Americans, and radical academics, it was the Great Depression of the 1930s that created the social upheaval that produced the social relevance of the folk songs of the period.

In 1929 millions became unemployed, and in the factories and mines that remained open, wages were cut and tightened policies affecting the rights of workers were instituted. In the South, textile and mine workers went on strike in Gastonia and Harlan in Kentucky. Stalinists from the northern United States went south to assist in organizing unions in Gastonia where they were subsequently introduced to southern folk songs. Southern folk songs coupled with revolutionary lyrics became central to workers' struggles. In 1929 Margret Larkin, a northern singer and writer of cowboy and wobbly, after being exposed to southern folk songs wrote, "the artist has the power to move people and thus accelerate the forward movement of history itself"; music can be used as a weapon. Referring to the power of protest music, Larkin noted: "what propaganda could better describe the infamy of the bosses" (Denisoff 1971, 18). Larkin was describing the role of folk music as the voice of the proletarian struggle of the 1920s and 1930s in the South at a time when workers often engaged in bloody battles against their bosses. Folk music was an effective tool in organizing workers because it was both simple and complex. It was simple in that it was easy to play and sing. It was generally complex in terms of its lyrical content, yet articulated in a way that was not too obtuse. This musical style was effective in generating emotional responses and urging workers to fight for their rights.

In the North, workers lacked a music style of their own. Northern Stalinists who spent time in the South organizing textile and mine workers brought back to the North, New York City in particular, southern folk music. This music traveled to other northern cities via musical groups like the Almanac Singers. Mass singing, a style based on the Russian model and the Stalinist movement, became the more popular workers' musical style in the North compared to the South. Mass singing, performed by workers' choruses, served to motivate large groups of workers as together they sang revolutionary songs. These songs included such southern folk tunes as the "ILD song" (International Labor Defense) and "Poor Miner's Farewell" (Denisoff 1971, 41). This style, during the 1920s and 1930s, was as popular as folk-singing trios and quartets in the 1960s. The revolutionary movement used the choruses to articulate the injustices of capitalism. Most of the material used by these groups was of European origin, although the Workers Music League (WML), a U.S.–based group, produced songs but with little success. The folk consciousness of the northern workers did, however, persist through the 1920s and into the 1930s. In response, workers' counter-movements also used mass singing to protect themselves against workers' movements. In fact, churches and congregations advanced religious teachings through music to persuade workers to be thankful for what they had and to wait for justice in the afterlife.

But both subversive and accommodative folk music, as a rural-based persuasive method, lost widespread appeal and political impact during the urbanization period of the United States, largely due to an increased number of foreign immigrants who had little knowledge or appreciation of rural America (Denisoff 1971). Consequently, during the 1930s until the social movements of the 1960s, folk music lost much of its influence on urban dwellers. But despite the downswing in this music style's popularity, an intriguing question remains: "Why would a movement dedicated to the education and politicization of the urban proletariat pick folk music (mass singing) as a propaganda tool?" (Denisoff 1971). The answer lies partly in the American Communist Party's belief at the time that folk music appealed to the urban proletariat's consciousness. After all, folk music is simple, free from commercialism, and capable of uniting the masses. It worked in Russia, so it was thought that it would work in the United States.

Yet the American Communist Party and other radical political movements lost sight of the fact that their rank and file were from other countries and spoke very little English beyond memorizing rote slogans and phrases. In addition, the unrelenting repression against labor and workers' movements did little to help organizers convince workers facing violence against them to stay the course. More important, the leadership of the labor movement by the 1940s was already becoming increasingly disconnected from their own rank and file, thus becoming ineffective in sustaining the movement's mobilization. But some argue that it was neither internal problems nor problems since then that were the main source of the movements' demise. It was U.S. capitalists backed by their government, who together conspired to demonize and make criminals, through effective use of the media (Chomsky & Herman 1988) and state-sanctioned violence and terror against those deemed a threat to the social order (Churchill & Vander Wall 1990a) that did the movements in. The U.S. government set up special agencies and passed laws in their fight against radicals.

In 1906 Attorney General Charles S. Bonaparte established the Bureau of Investigation (BoI) through a departmental order, against Congress's willingness to endorse the idea. In a statement to Congress about the BoI, Bonaparte stated, "a Department of Justice with no force of permanent police in any form under its control is assuredly not fully equipped for its work" (Churchill & Vander Wall 1990a, 17). In 1910, according to George Wickersham, head of BoI after Bonaparte:

> [The BoI is intended to enforce] the national banking laws, antitrust laws, peonage laws, the bucketshop law, the laws relating to fraudulent bankruptcies, the impersonation of government officials with intent to defraud, thefts and murders committed on government reservations, offenses committed against government property, and those committed by federal court officials and employees, Chinese smuggling, customs frauds, internal revenue frauds, post office frauds, violations of the neutrality act...land frauds and immigration and naturalization cases (Churchill & Vander Wall 1990a, 18).

By 1917 when the United States officially entered the war against Germany, the BoI was responsible for enforcing the newly enacted Espionage Act and the Alien Act designed to silence both U.S. citizens and noncitizens from speaking and acting out against the war and against the capitalist imperatives. The Alien Act was specifically designed to "exclude and expel from the United States aliens who are members of the anarchist classes" (Churchill & Vander Wall 1990a, 18).

For the BoI, this change resulted in an increase in allocated strength and power. One of the BoI's first targets was the Industrial Workers of the World (IWW), which had made substantial progress in organizing workers into "one big union" and which was also against the war. Over fifty key IWW organizers were arrested on false charges, convicted, and imprisoned for up to twenty years. The IWW was also fined more that $2,500,000. As a result, the IWW was destroyed.

After the war, the BoI needed an excuse to continue their work at eliminating opposition groups. Consequently, Attorney General A. Mitchell Palmer orchestrated an "anarchist" bombing campaign that included the bombing of government and corporate facilities and the spreading of anarchist literature around the bomb scene. As a result, a war on radicals dubbed the "Palmer Raids" ensued with public support. By the early 1920s the Palmer Raids, in the eyes of the state, sufficiently squashed dissent within the U.S. borders. Subsequently, J. Edgar Hoover, then BoI director, focused on restructuring the BoI, which would put it in the position of regulating national policy in coming years. The first thing Hoover did was to change the name from BoI to the Federal Bureau of Investigation (FBI), as a way of distancing itself from its own bad reputation. Hoover then fired people he deemed incompetent workers; increased wages; put in place a rigid, behaviorist, disciplinary code; and instilled a centrist organizational form that required everything anybody did be in the name of the director. The FBI continued collecting intelligence (information) on criminals and other undesirables through fingerprinting as well as through illegal operations like phone taps and bugs. In short, these tactics have and continue to be used on any group or individual deemed potentially threatening to the social order.

As outlined above, the U.S. federal government has been engaged in domestic counterintelligence functions at least since the days of the BoI through their efforts to discredit and destroy the IWW. During the 1940s and 1950s the Socialist Workers Party (SWP) and the Communist Party, USA (CPUSA) were the primary targets of the FBI's counterintelligence operations dubbed COINTELPROs. According to the former head of the Counterintelligence Division (CID), William C. Sullivan and Cartha D. "Deke" DeLoach, major players in the design of COINTELPRO, in referring primarily to the SWP and the CPUSA: "we were engaged in COINTELPRO tactics, to divide, conquer, weaken, in diverse ways, an organization in 1941" (Churchill & Vander Wall 1990a, 37). In sum, groups that have been victims of the FBI's COINTELPROs have included "socialists, communists, union organizers, black activists, anarchists and other 'ultra radicals'" (Churchill & Vander Wall 1990a, 27). Along with the squashed movements that supported it, folk music too was beaten out of the political arena.

By the mid-1950s, however, folk music began to regain popularity due in part to the career of the Weavers, though ill fated, who demonstrated the marketability of folk music. As a result of their mainstream success, the Weavers became professional musicians and no longer represented a class or movement (Denisoff 1971). After gaining mainstream success, *Sing Out!,* a Left-wing magazine, denounced the Weavers as representing the proletarian struggle. In addition, the Right, under McCarthyism, blacklisted the Weavers in 1952 putting an early end to their career. As musical historians have noted (Denisoff 1971), the significance of the Weavers was not in their longevity, but in that they demonstrated that folk music, accompanied by corporate polishings such as orchestras, was a salable commodity. Even more important was that the Weavers reaffirmed to former Almanac Singers and "People's songsters," whose music was the grass-roots music of the Left, labor, and political causes in the 1930s, that folk music was the music of America (Denisoff 1971).

Elvis Presley and Harry Belafonte also contributed to the rebirth of folk music, due largely to their outstanding stage performances coupled with their musical ability. Pete Seeger of the Weavers, however, was responsible for much of the popularity of folk music at colleges and universities. Because of Seeger's contempt of Congress, resulting in his being blacklisted, his performances were limited to "progressive summer camps, left-wing groups and politically tolerant colleges and universities" (Denisoff 1971, 157). The influence of Seeger is undoubtedly impossible to gauge, however he did "Keep the 'little light shining'" (Denisoff 1971, 158).

Riding on the successes of his antecedents, and on the rising social movements of the 1960s and 1970s, Bob Dylan brought folk music into the mainstream. The folk music revival of the 1960s, unlike its predecessors, flourished during a more economically lucrative historical period and was thus characterized by more co-optation through individual success because of the ability to sell records. Phil Ochs, one of the most controversial artists of the revival stated, "I'm only singing about my feelings, my attitudes, my views" (Denisoff 1971, 165). Tom Paxton, another controversial artist of the revival, stated "Every artist's first responsibility is to himself" (Denisoff 1971, 165). Bob Dylan on a number of occasions indicated that his first responsibility was himself, and that folk music was employed only to launch his career, not to change social structures. Many of these new mainstreamed folk musicians either lacked or had been stripped of the community-oriented ideology of their predecessors, yet they were still marketed and deemed by Left-wing journals such as *Sing Out!* as "Woody's children" (Denisoff 1971). Often presenting themselves as individualistic, musicians such as Bob Dylan, through their music, offered innovative, revolutionary, hybrid, counterhegemonic stances to a much wider audience through commercialism than their predecessors. What is more, the mainstream folk music of the 1960s was a thin veil covering a much more radical, even revolutionary, movement going on in the streets—a movement that was uniting progressive whites, African Americans, and Chicanos/as, and was thus deemed extremely dangerous to the social order. The FBI's response to the Black Panther Party (BPP) is representative. According to Ward Churchill:

> By the fall of 1968, the FBI felt it had identified the organization most likely to succeed as the catalyst of a united black liberation movement in the U.S. This was the BPP...On September 8, 1968, J. Edgar Hoover let it be known in the pages of the *New York Times* that he considered the Panthers 'the greatest [single] threat to the internal security of the country.' Shortly thereafter, William Sullivan sent the accompanying memo to George C. Moore, outlining a plan by which already-existing COINTELPRO actions against the BPP might 'be accelerated' (Churchill & Vander Wall 1990b, 123).

The FBI couldn't just attack the BPP and black, working-class communities in general without the support from those outside of those communities.

In other words, white and black middle-class folks had to believe that the BPP was a threat to national security for the FBI to be able to justifiably wage war on them. However, as we now know, the BPP did not instigate violence, they were not terrorists, but they did support self-defense, which was distorted by the FBI in cahoots with the mainstream media to discredit and criminalize the BPP. In the words of Huey P. Newton, minister of defense, BPP: "We will defend ourselves against attack and against aggression. But overall, we're advocating the end to all wars" (Newton 1969, quoted in Foner 1995, 70).

To justify repression, the FBI had to report to the media that the BPP was communistic, socialist, antidemocratic, racist (antiwhite and anti-Semitic), 'violence prone,' conducting 'physical attacks on police' and making 'efforts to perpetuate violence in the United States'" (Churchill & Vander Wall 1990b, 123). In the words of Bobby Seale, chairman, BPP, "we want some land, some bread, some housing, some education, some clothing, some justice, and some peace" (Seale 1969, quoted in Foner 1995, 80). According to Assata Shakur (1987), former BPP member, "the first thing the enemy tries to do is isolate revolutionaries from the masses of people, making us horrible and hideous monsters so that our people will hate us" (p. 181).

The BPP's Ten-Point Platform and Program speaks directly to the democratic imperative versus the capitalist imperative. Consider the words of David Hilliard, chief of staff, BPP: "we must remember this country is run by a slave oligarchy and brigandish criminals who have no respect for its people, be they Black or White; its primary interest is capitalism" (1969, quoted in Foner 1995, 122). Similarly, in 1969 Bobby Seale highlights the democratic imperative central to the BPP's focus. Consider his words:

> In the last few years, on every major college campus, murderous, brutal fascism in America made its appearance against White, Black, and Brown students and other students who attempted to use their basic 'democratic rights' to change racist administrations...and protest poverty in the ghettos in America (1969, quoted in Foner 1995, 79).

Because of their push for democracy, not because of their supposed use of violence, the BPP was deemed a threat to U.S. hegemony.

In this environment, people struggling for justice began to organize themselves in different ways. But despite the social movements of the 1960s and 1970s, which were constantly under virtual attack, the movements and the music of the time was co-opted by mainstream forces. As a reaction to this trend, other movements began to emerge in a number of communities. A small group of African Americans in Philadelphia during the 1970s organized themselves according to the teachings of naturalist John Africa calling themselves MOVE, which means to be in harmony with all who live, which exists on a move. Although many have either been killed or jailed, MOVE members remain strong and committed, serving as a powerful example of uncompromising revolutionary struggle.

In white middle- and working-class communities, punk rock was also born though largely influenced by African American rock and roll. According to Laing (1985), the term *punk* was not used until 1972 or 1973 by small fanzines to describe "garage bands" that sounded like bands of the 1960s that were no longer around because they lacked talent. According to Greg Shaw, founder of Bomp Magazine, a rock and rock fanzine, looking back on the early 1970s:

> Punk rock in those days was a quaint fanzine term for a transient form of mid-'60s music considered so bad (by the standards of the time) that it was a joke to the 'critics' who made their living analyzing the neuroses of Joni Mitchell (Laing 1985, 13).

Punk in this light, served in part to revitalize "lost legions of past popular music" (Laing 1985, 13). Shaw's statement also credits the naming of punk to semi-underground fanzines, not by the mainstream critics such as *Rolling Stone* (Laing 1985). Rock critic Ellen Willis notes "punk was not used generically until the early seventies when critics began applying it to unregenerate rock-and-rollers with an aggressively lower-class style…" (Laing 1985, 12).

Much of punk's aggressive lower-class style and stance focused on a disgust and distrust of mainstream conceptions of musicality and style. According to a number of music scholars (Dancis 1978; Laing 1985; McDonald 1987; DeMott 1988; Davies 1994) punk was, in part, a response to traditional mainstreamed rock and roll and a conservative political environment. However, as indicated earlier, skateboarding countercultures in the United States have had significant influences on both the emergence and continuation of punk rock, an aspect of punk that music scholars have neglected. Such investigation on the role of skateboarding on punk rock music as well as punk rock countercultures in general is the focus of Chapter 4 (pp. 61-64). More important to this chapter, however, is the political atmosphere in which punk emerged. It was a period during the 1970s when racist politics began to predominate, and when the system of redistributing income in the United States began to break down on a scale similar to that of the Great Depression (Albelda et al. 1988).

The breakdown of income redistribution in the United States, according to Albelda et al. (1988), can be explained by three developments. First, the social institution of marriage that began and continues to change. More and more women began entering the labor force only to be stuck in "pink collar" jobs with incomes significantly lower than their male counterparts. "Second, the U.S. economy suffered a long-term decline in its overall performance" during the 1970s (Albelda et al. 1988, 13). This decline, which started in the early 1970s, was marked by economic stagnation that continued into the 1980s with Reagan's trickle-down economics. Finally, the conservative economics of the late 1970s and 1980s, known as Reaganomics, increased taxes on the poor further impoverishing women and minorities, while simultaneously increasing the wealth of the already disproportionately wealthy white male. The preceding factors essentially resulted in the breakdown of a socially oriented economic system characteristic of the 1960's war on poverty, and replaced it with a system that led to the explosion of poverty and inequality on a national level that continues to exist today. The punk rock stance emerged from under the rubble of the conservative backlash against the 1960s and the so-called socialist liberal war on poverty programs.

However, it is important to say that punk rock does not have obvious musical roots. From African American–based rhythm and blues, rock and roll emerged in the post–World War II 1950s as the music of white working- and middle-class youth resistance. However, rock and roll has been co-opted by the dominant culture, largely a result of multinational record companies buying out small punk labels. Punk rock is rock and roll taken to another level. Youth subcultures have upped the stakes with Mohawk haircuts and leather, so as to keep conservatives from co-opting it, though today punk rock is a hot commodity often promoted by retail companies as a new dress fad. Unlike traditional rock and roll and the folk consciousness described above, punk rock is generally a much more angry, violent, sexist, and often racist form of musical resistance. However, like folk music, punk rock is part of workers' struggles; though largely male and white in its origin, it is not exclusively so.

Many white middle-class youth got involved in punk as well as other subversive genres as discussed by Donna Gaines in *Teenage Wasteland* (1991) for a number of reasons. Gaines documents how many middle-class suburban youth are dissatisfied with and feel rejected by dominant society and thus reject their prescribed roles, and are therefore labeled and self-identify as "burnouts."

In other words, many youths who reject their prescribed roles wind up destroying themselves in their attempts at destroying their roles. The self-destructive, suicidal burnouts Gaines studied primarily listen to and identify with heavy metal music, which serves as a common identity they feel accepted in and belong to, much the same way punk does. This music serves as the basis of their (our) organic knowledge and thus unmaterialized revolutionary potential, and provides them with a group to be accepted by, which is extremely important to them in an otherwise cold and distant world.

Racial and ethnic minorities and women have also contributed to the creation and re-creation of the alternative cultural spaces and stances of punk rock, although their numbers have traditionally been small. Despite punk rock's white male heterosexual roots, an increasing number of queer punks are developing their own scene (Fenster 1992). Yet as long as practitioners are not too radical or experimental, like many queer punks, multinational record companies will work to commodify and exploit them by buying them out because of the potential marketability (Laing 1985). Once bought, corporations like Sony and Time/Warner, if necessary, force their corporate image on practitioners, thus watering them down. These corporate criminals, as viewed by punks, thus turn subversion into vehicles of legitimation for their own corporate interests. But as Paulo Freire (1970b) emphasizes, while human creativity can be limited, it can never be totally destroyed, so subversive elements of punk rock music remain alive even within the most conservative corporations.

By changing the meaning of the punk stance so that it appeals to a young conservative population, corporations undermine the very reasons that punk emerged, namely to reject prescribed roles and to protest the deleterious effects of capitalism. As a result, the capitalist imperative, where nothing is not for sale, has kept punk localized. In other words, only the most radical and experimental and thus new forms of punk tend not to be absorbed into the mainstream (Laing 1985). Because capitalists will eventually attempt to profit from everything, and because what's new today will not be new tomorrow, innovation has been and continues to be a significant characteristic of the punk rock stance. In fact, despite the commercialization of punk, which has had debilitating effects on its community-based ties, and thus its ability to forge alliances with other groups, punks have not been stopped from subverting the music industry and society as a whole.

Undermining the effects of multinational corporations on punk, as outlined above, is supported by an individual we will refer to as "Mike," the owner of a

Los Angeles–based recording studio who has been producing punk bands for eighteen years, including Black Flag, The Minutemen, The Meat Puppets, Husker Du, the Descendents, and Penny Wise, just to name a few. Over the years Mike claims he has recorded his share of "hairspray" bands in order to, monetarily, be able to do the work he feels is important, which is providing punk bands the opportunity to cut records. Mike expressed particular interest in being able to provide those punk bands, who would not otherwise be able to make records, with ridiculously low studio rates, free rates, or studio time in exchange for services, like painting for him. However, there have been punkers who at one time were impoverished, but ended up on MTV making fat cash for multinational corporations, for whom Mike expressed extreme dislike, for being "sellouts" and supporting "corporate dogs' appetites."

According to Mike, when punk bands achieve financial success, meaning becoming multimillionaires (which Mike defined as when they "make the corporate dogs drool"), they *always* lose their community base and individual ties. Examples given were Green Day and The Offspring. Entering the mainstream, according to Mike, does not necessarily equal financial success. For example, Penny Wise has entered the mainstream, but only makes a modest living and maintains their resistant stance within boundaries of mainstream cultural spaces. Because of what raw punk is—too radical and experimental for the mainstream—in eighteen years of recording punk bands, Mike claims that when punk bands achieve mainstream success it seems to be indicative of corporate acceptance and the rejection of punk rock ideals. Mike has yet to see a punk band remain punk after corporate success. Punk is a form of music created for kids by kids as a means of expressing their anger and frustration with dominant society and the roles prescribed to them as workers, as men, as whites, and so forth. According to Mike, it is conceptually impossible to be a punk millionaire. Yet Mike shared a story, which was an example of how Penny Wise has entered the mainstream but continues to perpetuate the general punk attitude. The story goes something like this: A few weeks ago the band was in his studio doing some recording, and a member of the band received a phone call from a credit card company. The credit card company representative wanted this particular member of Penny Wise to make some type of payment toward his credit card bill. The band member told the credit card company representative that the company would never see his money, and that he didn't care if he ever had a credit card again because "I'm a punk rocker, fuck you." The attitude/value/stance described as punk is thus "fuck the mainstream," which is also a way of life. Mike described Penny Wise as "real," in that they "lead the life to the fullest." Some punk bands that make it big lose their "I don't give a fuck" attitudes and concern themselves with maintaining an image in order to make money and placate corporate dogs. For example, Henry Rollins, one-time member of Black Flag, according to Mike, is now "just a fucking movie star, a sellout and fuck him."

According to Mike on the origins of punk, "it has always been here and it will always be here." There have and will always be kids who want to tell the whole world to "fuck off and die," who could care less about musical mastery or materialism. However, it was bands like Black Flag and the Dead Kennedys who made thrashing aggression popular enough that it was named "punk rock." Contrary to Mike's assessment, however, DeMott (1988) and other scholars argue that punk rock emerged in London after World War II as discussed earlier.

Punk rock emerged among the working-class youth subculture known as *skins*. They were characterized by working-class concepts of masculinity, hardness, and working-classness. Their attire had symbolic meaning that was an amalgam of aspects borrowed from their own working-class culture—shaved heads borrowed from prisons, heavy work boots and short pants borrowed from predominantly male working-class occupations (DeMott 1988). One thing is true—punk emerged as a subversive youth movement. Nonetheless, the question still to be addressed; regardless of punk's origins or lack thereof, how much of punk serves to subvert dominant society and how much of it serves to perpetuate dominant values both today and yesterday? These are central questions in our analysis of punk. We therefore turn to previous studies done on punk rock that offer additional insight into the subversive versus accommodating dimensions of punk rock music in general.

Previous Academic Studies

Amy Mohan and Jean Malone published a study in 1994 titled "Popular Music as a 'Social Cement': A Content Analysis of Social Criticism and Alienation in Alternative-Music Song Titles." Mohan and Malone's focus was on the value system music communicates to its audience, which, when successful, acts as a "social cement." The authors hold that the value system that punk music, currently known as alternative music, communicates is "social criticism and alienation" (p. 288). Mohan and Malone looked, for purposes of comparison, to see how alternative music retained punk values to determine how much of these values are embodied by mainstream popular music. If alternative music does contain these values and mainstream music does not, then it would be possible to define the alternative community as more dissatisfied with the status quo and conventional social values than mainstream music.

Mohan and Malone's (1994) sample consisted of song titles from 1990 to 1992 and was drawn from:

> The music industry weekly Billboard published from January 6, 1990, to October 3, 1992. Song titles were taken from the 'Modern Rock Tracks' chart, a top 30 listing for alternative music, and the 'Hot 100' chart, a mainstream chart....A total of 343 alternative and 345 mainstream titles were included in the sample (p. 291).

As expected, they found that alternative music titles rated higher in the "social commentary" category than the mainstream titles, and that mainstream titles rated higher in the "love/romance" category. Alternative titles rated higher in the "negative event" category, as expected, but the same as mainstream titles in the "positive event" category, contrary to their expectations. The results showed that alternative music is higher in social criticism and alienation than mainstream music. Dave Laing reported similar findings in his book *One Chord Wonders: Power and Meaning in Punk Rock* (1985).

Dave Laing's (1985) study compared "the subject matter of the lyrics on the debut albums of the first five punk groups to achieve prominence in 1976–7, with the Top 50 best-selling singles in Britain in 1976" (p. 27). The results show a divergence between punk and mainstream rock lyrics in 1976. The results suggest that songs from the Top 50 deal more with dominant values such as romantic and sexual relationships, music and dance, which make up 86% of the Top 50 content versus 28% of punk content. By comparison, 65% of the punk albums were concerned with sexuality, social and political commentary, and first-person feelings contrary to the 7% of Top 50 lyrics.

Similarly, in 1987 James R. McDonald published a study titled "Suicidal Rage: An Analysis of Hardcore Punk Lyrics," which as the title suggests, focused on lyrical content. This study did not employ content analysis or any other scientific method for lyrical analysis, but it does focus on the lyrical content of some of the most hardcore punk of the late 1980s. McDonald makes the argument that hardcore punk is a directed rage against those in positions of power. According to McDonald, punk singers "focused their lyrics on social and political subjects" (p. 160) and that punk "is a grass-roots movement, and a political challenge to the existing order in government as well as in music" (p. 68). Making the argument that punk is an organized struggle, McDonald notes that "the common thread that continues to run through punk is a dissatisfaction with the modern world. How that frustration is articulated varies greatly" (p. 30).

In his analysis McDonald primarily focuses on the lyrics of the Suicidal Tendencies, The Vandals, and The F.U.'s—all based in southern California as white-boy bands. McDonald offers a definition of hardcore punk, which serves to guide his analysis. We use his definition at length because it highlights a general punk stance represented throughout this piece and gives voice to the lived experiences of many self-identified punkers. Consider McDonald's words:

> Hardcore is, as its name implies, hard in that it does not vary from the core of rock—that is, hardcore disavows commercialism, synthetic technological effect such as synthesizers, etc., the recording industry itself, and anything similar to the characteristics of mainstream rock. Albums are released in small numbers and are produced by very low-budget record companies. Morthland indicates that most hardcore albums cost less than $6,000 to record and most releases make a profit. The basic concept is that anyone can play, the tempo is always very fast, approaching a hectic, monotonous pounding with little variation, and most importantly, the lyrics are not sung, but normally shouted, groaned or spoken—often by the audience in a concert setting as much as by the singer of a group. There exists then, none of the smooth vocal harmonies apparent in mainstream rock. The positioning of the hardcore vocalist is that of the leader of a mob—he/she must shout to be heard. This vocal intensity is transmitted on hardcore albums and accounts for the difficulty in transcribing the lyrics (p. 124).

McDonald's definition describes punk rock as authentic, symbolic, collective action free from mainstream influences. However, McDonald's conception of punk is what Giroux and Simon (1989) would identify as a one-sided perspective, not acknowledging the complexities of social reality (discussed more in Chapter 4, pp. 61-64).

Nonetheless, McDonald's definition of punk does paint a relatively accurate picture of what goes on in a typical punk musical performance/experience, regardless of political orientation, in its pure form and unfettered by commercialization. If punk bands do make it into the mainstream, as suggested earlier by punk music producer Mike, their performances tend to drastically change, widening the gap between performer and consumer. Consequently, punkers lose their community-based ties and thus lose the very essence that made them punk.

According to Dave Laing (1985), punk rock is characterized by three forms of hostility to the mainstream music scene:

> The 'do it yourself' attitude which refused to rely on the institutions of the established music industry, whether record companies or music press; a challenge to the orthodoxy of 'artistic excellence' in punk's choice of musical style; and the aggressive injunction of new subject-matter into the lyrics of popular songs, some of which broke existing taboos (p. 14).

That is why punk rock according to Laing's (1985) definition, operates exclusively outside of the mainstream, though some punk music producers like Mike would disagree. It is not surprising then that the lines between audience and performers are not always as distinguishable or important in punk as they are in mainstream rock and roll. As Laing (1985) notes "the cover of 'Sniffin' Glue 1' announced itself to be 'For Punks.' It was the first time that the audience rather than the music had been defined in that way" (p. 15). Punk music and punk communities/individuals represent each other. The line between punk practitioner and consumer is thus often virtually indistinguishable to those outside the genre. However, the line between punk rock and mainstream rock is not always clear, even to those operating inside the punk genre. For example, Bad Religion is a punk band that has been making music since the early 1980s and has experienced mainstream success; some punkers consider them punk while others do not. Punk lyrics, however, do portray particular messages that, according to the research cited above, do represent those who listen to them. How then do individuals respond to the messages perpetuated by these types of popular cultural forms?

A study done by Bennett and Ferrell in 1987 titled "Music Videos and Epistemic Socialization" utilizes content analysis, deconstruction, and cultural hermeneutics in an attempt to identify the "common knowledge" created in part by popular culture, and music videos in particular. Though this study did not analyze the lyrics of music or even punk rock in general, it did speak to the question: What impact does music have on those who listen to it?

More generally, the purpose of the study was to redefine how an audience responds to popular culture and analyze its impact on those who, in this case, view it. In so doing, the authors developed the term *epistemic socialization*, which refers to events that establish "first principles," meaning what individuals refer to when questions arise. Accordingly, events the individual experiences ultimately shape their actions by discriminating against what is known to be possible and impossible. What the authors argue is that popular culture similar to social institutions such as families, peer groups, schools, churches, and so forth, perpetuate events of epistemic socialization. The authors concluded that: "Popular music recordings—audio or video—have a place in the common cognitive careers of their audiences" (Bennett & Ferrell 1987, 346). The messages transmitted through lyrics in this light influence how individuals view and react to the world in which they live. And though, as previously stated, punk rock, like the music industry in general, is male dominated, women have not only impacted the music industry but punk as well. In concluding this chapter, we turn to a study focusing on the experiences of women in music.

A chapter published in *Feminist Messages* (1993) by Cheryl Keyes titled "'We're More Than a Novelty, Boys': Strategies of Female Rappers in the Rap Music Tradition," while not focused on punk rock in particular, does offer some insight on how women have used music to both subvert and accommodate dominant male society. Keyes holds that women rappers, like their male counterparts, rap about inner-city life but offer a women's perspective. Despite their presence, according to Keyes, women rappers are viewed as inferior to their male counterparts, whether other rappers or record producers. Thus, in order to compete with male rappers, Keyes argues, female rappers must embody the male aesthetic. The male aesthetic becomes necessary not only to be produced, but also to be heard. Thus, messages in female rappers' rhymes often accommodate male-dominated society. Traditionally, women rappers have to not only embody the male aesthetic, but their raps have to be written by men in order for producers, disproportionately male, to even listen to them. Keyes quotes Princeta, a female rapper whom she interviewed: "only when I lead them [male rap producers] to believe that a man had written or produced my stuff did they show interest [in recording me]" (p. 204). That accommodating, according to Keyes, is a means to an end.

By following what Keyes calls "male rules," women can enter rap as performers, and then are able to create social space for their own "woman-centered" perspectives. Keyes argues that women use rap for empowerment by presenting the marginalized status of women in a patriarchal society and then challenge it by reversing gender roles in their raps. Keyes notes that women rappers reverse gender roles by presenting men at the mercy of women. Another strategy Keyes argues women rappers employ is when they present rap as genderless, but at the expense of covering up their feminist messages. Keyes never states what that feminist message is or provides any examples. She does make reference to Yo-Yo, a woman rapper who organized the Intelligent Black Women's Coalition, which was a response to the rap industry's ongoing sexism and misogynist lyrics in rap. In doing so, women rappers "speak for the empowerment of women..." (Keyes 1993, 216). Despite the recognition that there are women rappers whose messages are perpetuated in song, women rappers have largely been left out of discussions on rap. The same is argued here in relation to punk.

Conclusion

White male scholars for the most part have used content analysis to quantify and make generalizations about popular music lyrics dating back to 1941 (Adorno 1989; Arato & Gebhardt 1989). After a period of almost exclusively focusing on romantic love and boy-girl relationships in the 1940s and 1950s, scholars in the 1960s, in response to the popular music of the 1960's social movements, began looking at social protest as a dominant message in popular music. However, an in-depth analysis of sex, gender, and race/ethnicity has been and continues to be largely excluded from academic studies of music lyrics. We attempt to address this gap in our discussion of punk music and culture.

Chapter 4
Skateboarding and Punk Rock: The Connection

As indicated in Chapter 2 (pp. 15-40), the skateboarding community has had a significant impact on the emergence and continuation of a large portion of the punk rock scene throughout the United States. In my (Curry Malott's) experiences with punk rock, skateboarding has been an inseparable element. Since at least my freshman year of high school (1986), if not before, I have considered myself in some way or another to be a skaterpunk (now a self-identified skaterpunkhippiehiphopper). What follows is an analysis of the interconnectedness of punk rock and skateboarding—a continuation of my definition of punk rock, largely based on my lived experiences.

Sk8in' 'n' Destroyin'

Previous research on skateboarding has primarily focused on skaters' redefining the primary function of public geographical locations, such as using hand-rails and steps as skating obstacles rather than for walking up or down (Austin & Willard 1998). The ability to redefine public spaces speaks to the power relationships citizens have with their state, and indeed is an important aspect of skateboarding. But more importantly, how skaters have come to view themselves—in opposition to dominant society—and how their actions both resist and accommodate the hegemony of dominant societies is important to this study. I focus on my own experiences and theories about those experiences to illustrate our points.

For many young white men like myself, punk rock and skateboarding have been and continue to be vehicles through which counterhegemonic ideas are articulated and countercultural spaces are created. As outlined above, this cultural space is not unfamiliar to me. I came of age in the 1980s in Oregon and in Ohio, and actively participated within the countercultural spaces of the skaterpunks. As a result, I went through something similar to the process of conversion described by Snow and Phillips (1980) in a critical analysis of cults and their recruitment processes. For myself, conversion into the skaterpunk counterculture meant rejecting particular aspects of dominant society (discussed in Chapter 4, pp. 61-64) on the grounds that it is corrupt and has debilitating effects on the self and our communities in general, a dominant theme in the messages of punk rock music (Dancis 1978; Laing 1985; DeMott 1988; Davies 1994). How have punk rock and skateboarding coalesced in particular spaces of the U.S. landscape resulting in the widespread countercultures of skaterpunks?

> Every once in a while I wonder about what ever happened to certain skaters. I picture a lot of them not even skating anymore and being just a regular person with a regular job doing regular things. I guess I see them all grown up into droning adults....Thankfully, there are some that refuse the social pressures to grow up into the model adult and do what they really want to do regardless of what others may think or say. One large example of this is Duane Peters. One of the reasons why the public at large hates skateboarders is due to Duane. He helped usher in the snotty, punk rock style, aggression and attitude to a sport that was bound up in nut hugging O.P. shorts with an Olympic future while rocking out to 'Fleetwood Mac' or 'The Eagles.' Since then it seemed natural to assume that if you skated, you were a punk... (Franklin 1996, 1).

According to Franklin (1996), white, male punkers co-opted skateboarding in the late 1970s, thus extending the pool of potential punks.

To understand punk is to understand that punk rock emerged as a result of a general boredom, disgust, and rejection of mainstream culture (Biafra 1997). Skateboarding was originally part of mainstream culture, but, like rock and roll, was co-opted by individual punkers as a viable avenue of simultaneously expressing and creating their cultural identity, which centered around a general dislike of post–civil rights, backlash, mainstream, and U.S. consumer-based society (Biafra 1997). At the grass-roots level, the skaterpunk community, in my experience, serves as a kind of new social movement or counterculture where punk rock is the ideological tool that connects skaters across the country to advance new ideas creating active discourse between punkers via music[1] and fanzines[2]—the do-it-yourself (DIY), as cheaply as possible, punk philosophy.

In my experience, most skaterpunks are either primarily devoted skaters who listen to punk (fans) or devoted punk musicians who sometimes skate. However, there are individuals who are both active professional skaters as well as active recording punk rockers, such as Duane Peters. Duane Peters is a professional skater and lead singer of the punk rock bands, the U.S. Bombs and the Hunns. Peters represents the hardcore, aggressive, antiauthority attitude and at the same time the heterosexism and homophobia typical of the skaterpunk counterculture. The homophobia Peters frequently expresses was captured in an interview response to snowboarding: "[t]here's so many queers in Huntington that just turn me off" (Doggin 1996, 2). Peters also is known to have expressed anti-homophobic messages at his shows by explaining to the crowd how he believes that he figured out why they had come to the show: "to fuck, man and woman, or man and man, or woman and woman, it's the 1990s, it's a PC world, so whatever you want, but we are here to fuck" (Peters 1999).

Duane Peters used to skate for Beer City skateboards (he now rides for Black Label) and records on Beer City's label Beer City Records (and also now on Hell Cat, which is part of Epitaph, as well as his own Disaster records). Beer City is an example of a company started and maintained by punks for punks. The irony is that Beer City, among other similar companies, also exists and operates within the established for-profit music scene, the very system punks attempt to subvert. Companies like Beer City work within the system as a means of getting their messages out and making a living—or simply *survivance.* But in the end, because they participate in the system to get their music out, they sometimes produce bands that perpetuate the interests of the ruling class.

Skaterpunks on the street, however, exist on the margins and resist from outside the boundaries of dominant society. Thus, in their daily lives, many skaterpunks refuse to participate in dominant society by not seeking legitimate employment and living on the streets. However, the isolation can be counterproductive because being isolated distances them from spaces where they can form alliances with other groups to create broader coalitions for social change. Others work jobs to survive but disrupt the social order by not conforming to accepted modes of dress, patterns of speech, and forms of dialect, and use public and private spaces such as steps and handrails as skating spots and canvases for graffiti art. By simply being a punker and skating, both individually and collectively, skaterpunks resist dominant society. Still, other punks are on the streets because they have no other place to go. They symbolize the United States' abandoning of children and the country's overall poor populations (Giroux 1983).

In a sense, the lifestyle characteristic of skaterpunks as well as that of dominant society could be conceptualized in terms of a continuum where skaterpunks are at one extreme—the radical Left and dominant society is at the other extreme the conservative Right. Skaterpunks tend to be relatively extreme because, by definition, countercultures are measured against the norms of dominant society; the further away on the continuum countercultures exist the more marginalized they are. The pressure of living on the margin sometimes takes its toll. It is because skaterpunks have a tendency to be extreme, and because the pressures to conform work so well that there is a high turnover rate. A producer I interviewed over the phone in Los Angeles, Mike, told me that it is because punk is so high energy and radical that bands don't usually stay together for long because "it is hard to maintain that level" of hardcore rage characteristic of punkers.

This high turnover rate also makes punk susceptible to co-optation because it suggests that it is not a cohesive movement and therefore easily infiltrated. For example, at times the most influential punk is predominantly ideologically aligned with Leftist politics while at other times geared more toward postmodernist defeatism, or even at times Right-wing conservatism (Davies 1994). The punk style has been co-opted and rearticulated as something different and foreign to the punk scene; that is, the Gen-X, slacker styles for sale at the mall. In addition, the conservative, positive image of skateboarding has recently become widespread in the mass media as evidenced by the X Games, commercials against kids smoking shown before movies at popular theatres and on TV, and through white, male middle-class, straight, skating legends. Such messages cleanse skateboarding of any of its counterhegemonic roots. Like punk rock in general, when skaters are portrayed as counterhegemonic, they are portrayed as slackers or Gen-Xers devoid of any real meaning or purpose.

Conclusion

Although we do not consider Beer City's label to be influential enough in the punk scene in general to be one of the primary labels for the content analysis portion of this study, it is an example of the impact skateboarding has had on punk rock and punk rock on skateboarding. Skateboarding might not be overtly noticeable in its influence on the music we analyze in the content analysis presented in later chapters of this book, but if it were not for skateboarding, punk rock might not be what it is today—an increasingly hybrid, multicultural, potentially revolutionary form of human expression.

Chapter 5
The Problem with the Larger Context

What follows is a content analysis of the lyrics presented by punk rockers; mostly white men (though some white women), African American men, and Latino men appear on the three record labels chosen. We are interested in uncovering the lyric message patterns as they developed over time, by decade in particular in order to identify what messages were prevalent at specific historical moments in time and presented by whom. The justification for the three record labels we used is discussed later in the sampling methods (Chapter 6, pp. 69-87). We are only interested in the messages people have received and continue to receive in the United States related to punk, despite the previously outlined differentiations made between U.S. and British punk. The population for this study is therefore primarily composed of punk rock produced within the United States as evidenced by the releases on the three chosen record labels.

Various demographic indicators are employed to differentiate lyrical messages. We assume that one's gender, race/ethnicity, among other variables such as class and sexuality, though not measurable in this study, informs how one both experiences and is experienced by the world (Freire 1970b; Tatum 1997; Lopez 1996) that situates individuals in ways that could potentially affect lyrical messages. For example, a black man in the United States is likely to have different life experiences and is experienced by the world substantially differently than a white man. That is not to say that all black males in the United States experience life the same way. However, a white man in the United States would not experience the racism a black man in the United States experiences. In addition, messages perpetuated by women punkers and men punkers will be differentiated based on the disparate roles men and women have occupied in this genre and society at large, as outlined previously. Furthermore, because punk rock is traditionally performed by white males it is also our interest to note what women and nonwhites have contributed to punk as punk rock performers across time. Unfortunately, content analysis produces typifications and generalizations as research results that flatten out the minute variations between individuals and within categories, and quite often create large-scale false differences between multiple categories. In an attempt to make up for some of the limitations of content analysis, and thus show the multidimensionalism of punk rock, we will include in this discussion some of the rich textures of message presenters' life experiences as punkers within the United States.

We will be looking at punk promoted by the three labels that comprise the population for this study in the 1980s and 1990s. In a recent issue of *Alternative Press* an interview appeared relevant to the historical context of punk employed in this study. Jello Biafra, a former Dead Kennedy as well as Lard singer and owner of Alternative Tentacles record label was the individual interviewed. The Dead Kennedys and Jello Biafra, both out of San Francisco, helped define and create the punk rock movement in the early 1980s. Jello Biafra is still making punk rock available through Alternative Tentacles and his continued involvement as a punk rocker (Mr. Microphone) in Lard. The article in its entirety puts punk in the United States in an historical context from the perspective of a punk rocker relevant to this study, so the majority of the article will be included.

In response to the 1970s, as Biafra (1997) states:

> I came of age in the '70s, and believe me, it was so miserable I nearly became a teen-suicide statistic. All the promise of rebellion and the breaking down of sexual mores of the '60s was dumped down to fern bars and escapist, hanging-plant, new-age apathy; horrible music like The Eagles, Chick Corea and Saturday Night Fever. It was a terrible time to come of age, and me and my friends said, 'Can you imagine a time so horrible that people would actually be nostalgic for the '70s?' We all agreed: 'No, it could never happen' (p. 96).

In response to the 1980s and 1990s' Biafra (1997) states:

> The '80s were probably worse [than the 1970s], except for the music. The self-centered apathy of the '70s became outright greed in the '80s. Now we see corporations trying to build up a whole new group of people even greedier than the Reagan democrats were, and calling them 'the Cocktail Nation.' You know, retro renaissance: Smoke cigars, play golf, refer to women as money in your slang terms at the bar (p. 96).

In response to retro and the "Elks Club," Biafra (1997) states:

> Oh, yeah. Remember all the lawsuits against the 'Elks Club' for not admitting women and non-whites? If you can't get 'em to do it by force and threats, at least you can get them to do it by dumb trends. [laughs.] I think any kind of retro is poison, and 'Fonzieism'[1] is particularly annoying and dangerous. Some of the people I see now who

run around with the logo of a band that broke up 15 years ago on the back of a leather jacket they bought at the mall last week, that isn't punk to me. They're punk Fonzies.

A lot of these self-described 'old-school punk' bands are so goddamned uninspired and boring. I mean, when we were helping invent the stuff, there wasn't any goddamn school with a bunch of teachers and rules. We were blowing up the school—the school known as '70s boredom. We were united in a common enemy: *Happy Days*, Boston, The Doobie Brothers and anything on Asylum Records. Yes, David Geffen has been poisoning this country with bad music for many years now (p. 96).

In response to why 1970's rock is coming back after twenty years, Biafra (1997) states:

I think the major labels have been salivating over it for years: 'Wow! We sure hoodwinked 'em and raked in the dough on Lynyrd Skynyrd before. Why not [create] a bunch of flannelled, espresso-fueled Skynyrd wannabes? People fell for it last time; let's do it again! And for that matter, we could bring back Saturday Night Fever with piercings and tattoos and call it 'electronica.'

I mean, some of it actually is very deliberate on the major labels' part because the multinationals that own those labels have to use all their entertainment companies as propaganda outlets to keep people stupid. But I don't think they were prepared for the political smarts that people like Nirvana, L7, and, yes, Pearl Jam brought into the mainstream. The only reason they let those bands out of the bag to begin with was so that a whole generation of white suburban kids wouldn't get their entire political brain food from rap music. 'We can't have them listening to this 'negro' music, so we'll give them some loud guitar music besides metal.'

The majors really didn't know what to do at first: 'Oh, my god, there's a whole new generation of people who really aren't interested in what Eric Clapton and Bob Seager are doing these days. Well, here's how to dumb down these kids—hand them a bunch of '70s clones with louder guitars, make sure the ones we sign have the most self-absorbed and stupid lyrics possible, and further water down the Nirvana Effect by dubbing their audience 'Generation X' and telling them all they're apathetic and hedonistic.'

Even if your music is '70s, the more relevant your lyrics are, the less likely you are to get signed to a major label. Instead, it's like, 'Boo-hoo. My girlfriend left me. I'm white and middle-class in the richest country in the world. I just got $1 million from Sony. Don't you feel sorry for me? Buy my record.' This is what they're trying to sell the people, and anyone who buys it is getting what they deserve. [laughs.] But not too many people have tried to document the history of people who came of age between the '60s and the '80s. We weren't dazed and confused; we were disgusted (p. 96).

Biafra highlights for us how music, like discourse in general, represents particular interests and worldviews whether the performer(s) are aware of it or not.

Following Biafra, then, punk rock, at its roots, represents a proactive part of the struggle for justice in U.S. society by naming, reflecting, and acting on that which is perceived to be unjust and inhumane. As a mouthpiece of social criticism throughout his career, Biafra has played a significant role in laying the foundations for a long-term political counterhegemonic movement. Punk rock, in this light, emerged and continues to exist as a response to a politically and socially conservative capitalist, white-supremacist ruling-class, a class with two branches—the Democrats and the Republicans. Whatever minor differences they may have, these parties are both designed to exploit and oppress all life—human, animal, marine, plant, all life—and have left vast amounts of land in the United States destroyed forever, including extinct animals and millions of humans locked away in federal penitentiaries and/or living in poverty. The data here will therefore be analyzed with reference to the dominant sociopolitical environments prevalent during the decades being analyzed, and will be situated in a historical context. The data analysis, which will include the analysis of individual lyrics, will look for particular themes in punk that correspond to particular political and social events at particular moments in time. Not to get caught up in Jello Biafra's optimistic perspective of punk outlined above, and thus lose our theoretical perspective, we will not only be looking for how punk has subverted conservative periods, but how it has supported them as well. We should note that the lyrics' message is the focus regardless of whether the messages were written by the presenters.

Chapter 6
Research Design: Why We Did What We Did

Content Analysis

The following is an overview of the methods used in analyzing some of the music themes discussed previously that have emerged in punk. *Content analysis* is a method employed by researchers in an attempt to study the "objective, systematic, and quantitative description of the manifest content of communication" (Holsti 1969, 3) whether written, auditory, visual, or an amalgam. Content analysis lends itself "for making replicable, valid inferences from data to their context" (Krippendorff 1980, 21). Scholars such as Holsti (1969) hold that objectivity is obtainable through content analysis by employing explicitly stated rules and procedures throughout the research process. However, a number of scholars (Peterson 1989; Grossberg et al. 1992) hold that complete objectivity is impossible no matter how strict and explicit research rules are, based on the inability of individuals to ignore their place in society and their own unique way of looking at the world. However, when coding manifest content, higher levels of objectivity and thus reliability are possible compared to the coding of latent content (Babbie 1995).

The coding of latent content allows one to achieve higher levels of validity compared to the coding of manifest content (Babbie 1995), though Holsti holds that latent content is not for the coding stage of research but for the inferential stage where the researcher draws conclusions from the results obtained through coding manifest content. However, as demonstrated by Mohan and Malone (1994), reliability is still an issue even when coding primarily manifest content. Because validity and deep meaning are important to this study, latent content has been coded, which has nevertheless allowed for the replication and thus the quantification of punk lyrical messages. Qualitative analysis was possible during the data analysis stage by providing in-depth analysis of particular lyrics that highlight the overall findings. As previously mentioned, a major focus of this study is to determine what percentage of messages articulated by men and women and white and nonwhite punk rockers have resisted dominant values and what percentage have accommodated dominant values at particular points in history.

Categories and Hypotheses

The theories outlined above on popular culture and the review of the literature on punk and rock and roll presented earlier were used to substantiate the variables we chose to measure. Like the rock and roll described by James T. Carey (1969b), we anticipate finding more *new values* than *old values* because punk rockers almost always write their own lyrics, unless they are doing a cover song. Besides the fact that it is too costly for small independent record companies to pay a professional songwriter to write lyrics, it is simply just not punk to have someone else write your lyrics, especially someone who represents the values of the dominant adult society. Carey (1969b) partly attributed the unconventional values predominant in the rock and roll lyrics he studied to the fact that they were largely written by the performers. Lyrics that perpetuate ideologies of dominant society are more likely written by someone other than the one singing them and not by rock and rollers (Carey 1969b).

Carey (1969b) measured old values versus new values articulated in popular song lyrics. Carey conceptualized old versus new values in the following way:

> Lyrics which are concerned with maximizing one's freedom in personal relationships and freeing one's self from societal constraints were categorized as lyrics representing newer values. They advocate or imply a more autonomous relationship between the sexes and/or criticize conventional society because of its misplaced values. Lyrics which enjoin explicitly or implicitly the acceptance of conventional values—for example, romantic notions about boy-girl relationships, fatalistic acceptance of the demands placed on one by the larger community, or expressing anxiety over social change—were classified as representing older values (p. 155).

Similarly, we are interested in measuring to what extent punk lyrics have accommodated dominant values (old values) and to what extent they have subverted dominant values (presence of new values).

We used Carey's (1969b) value concepts described above, but the categories were altered in order to represent the messages prevalent in punk discussed below. In addition, our decision to measure messages that accommodate dominant values and those that subvert dominant values is also based on the work of Giroux and Simon (1989) outlined earlier. Giroux and Simon (1989) suggest popular culture both enables and disables individuals in specific social contexts because of the multidimensional nature of struggles, contradictions, and re-formations in specific historical contexts.

The categories under the general theme of old values—sexism, racism, romantic love, homophobia, and antisocial protest—when present, we assume support the status quo by presenting white, presumably heterosexual men that support the system as superior to everybody else, and thus their predominance in positions of power is legitimated. Old values have therefore been employed to measure the accommodation of dominant society. The categories under the general theme of new values—social protest, antisexism, antiracism, rejection of romantic love, and the support of homosexuality—when present, we assumed to call into question the predominance of white, presumably heterosexual men in positions of power. We have therefore used new values to measure the subversion of dominant society. What follows are substantiations for the chosen categories.[1]

As suggested earlier, most studies since the 1970s that have analyzed the content of music lyrics have measured social protest in some way, shape, or form. Based on the work of Richard Cole (1971), we anticipate finding many punk lyrics containing social protest themes due to the fact that punk rock exists in the underground. Cole's study consisted of songs "of the annual top ten single songs during each year of the 1960s..." (p. 390). Cole found 10% of the songs in the second half of the decade had social protest themes. Cole inferred that if he had drawn his sample from more underground recordings, he would have found a higher percentage of social protest themes for, according to Cole, social protest was not a widely accepted theme in the mainstream during the 1960s and therefore existed outside of its boundaries. Similarly, Mohan and Malone (1994) found that alternative music was higher in social criticism than mainstream music because of its punk roots. Punk rock, according to Mohan and Malone (1994), embodies values that are dissatisfied with the status quo and conventional values. Laing (1985) found similar results concerning social criticism and punk rock.

Based on the writings of Dancis (1978), "Safety Pins and Class Struggle: Punk Rock and the Left" and Willis (1977), *Learning To Labor: How Working Class Kids Get Working Class Jobs,* outlined above, we expect to find sexist messages as a predominant theme in punk lyrics throughout its history. Dancis argued that sexism has existed in punk rock from its beginning in both the United States and Britain, and that punk is no better a place for women than traditional rock, and at times worse. In addition, based on the critiques we raised of Keyes' (1993) work, there should also be some sexist themes from women employing the male punk aesthetic for empowerment. Both men and women are therefore expected to perpetuate affirmations of oppression. However, based on Fenster (1992) as well as Curry Malott's extensive exposure to punk rock, we anticipate finding some women and some male queer punkers expressing antisexist views, however small a percentage this may be. In addition, Simon Frith (1982) has argued that because punk rock "rejected both romantic and permissive conventions, and refused in particular, to allow sexuality to be constructed as a commodity...punks opened up the possibility that rock could be against sexism" (pp. 243–244).

By contrast, racist messages will probably be less frequent than sexist messages, though not totally absent due in part to the labels that have been chosen for analysis. For example, Jello Biafra, owner of Alternative Tentacles, is a known radical lefty and would probably not sign bands that contradict his own politics, although according to Biafra, the bands on his label have complete artistic freedom. Dancis (1978) holds that punk rock has largely resisted being co-opted by racist political groups, such as the National Front, although a few bands have done racist songs such as the Nuns described above. We note, however, that Dancis was not only writing about British punk, but at a time when punk was first becoming a genre; a lot has happened sociopolitically since the late 1970s. Still, punk is largely performed by white males and as such is part of the status quo (Abu-Jamal 1996, 1997, 2000). Therefore, we expect to find white supremacy either being resisted or perpetuated.

Next, most if not all of the content analysis of music lyrics has measured some aspect of romance and/or sexual relationships due to the predominance of these themes in popular music. Carey (1969b) as well as Cole (1971), though to a lesser extent, found that love/romance themes had declined in popular music, rock and roll specifically, and that love/romance themes were less prevalent in rock and roll than in other forms of music. Laing's (1985) results showed that 21% of the punk lyrics he studied contained messages involving romance/sexual relationships while 60% of the Top 50 lyrics contained these themes. Mohan and Malone (1994) found that the alternative lyrics they sampled contained only 7.6% of love/romance themes while mainstream lyrics contained 22.9% of these themes. Consequently, we also measured love/romance assuming that earlier recordings would have greater amounts of love/romance themes. In sum, we were open to finding patterns similar to those found by Carey (1969a, 1969b), Cole (1971), Laing (1985), and Mohan and Malone (1994) in terms of love/romance because we are looking at a similar musical genre employing similar methodologies.

Finally, we measured homosexual content. Dancis (1978) identified the role of homosexuals in punk rock as practitioners in Britain during the 1970s. Fenster (1992), however, holds that homosexuals in punk rock in the United States have traditionally been in the closet because of the homophobia prevalent in punk, and have only recently come out as both practitioners and consumers of queer punk. Homophobia expressed by straight punkers has thus been and continues to be a dominant theme in punk rock.

In addition to the categories we outlined above, we included the category "absent," which will serve as a place to put songs that do not fit into any of the above-outlined categories. For example, if a song is coded as "absent" on all categories, it was considered "absent."

Operational Definitions

The next step was to develop a set of instructions or rules—a coding system—in order to systematically observe and record content from lyrics. These rules guided the categorization and classification of observations (Neuman 1994). Categories were constructed with the intention of mutual exclusivity. The variables were coded as either present (1) or absent (0). A method of inter-coding reliability was conducted in order to fine-tune the operationalization of the variables, which is discussed in greater detail in the "Coding" section. What follows are the conceptual and operational definitions of variables followed by instructions that guided the employment of the operational definitions. Note that based on the work of Brent Shea (1972), the categories were operationally defined by example. Shea's sample was drawn from the most popular songs in the United States from 1967 to 1970. "The categories were operationally defined by example" (p. iii). Trend analysis was employed to determine change over time as well as to compare previous cross-sectional content analysis. Consider the following definitions we used to code songs and keep in mind that they are the foundation of the next two chapters, "Results" and "Discussion."

1. The conceptual definition for social protest was based on the definition employed by Cole (1971), which served as the basis for the social criticism/ protest category.

> *Social protest*: It [is] expected that [punk] songs [will] manifest [many] references to social protest—defined as disapproval of situations existing in society or of attitudes widely

held or approval of attitudes not widely held [e.g. a protest against war or capitalism, endorsing revolution, dropping out of the system economically, etc.] (p. 391).

The singer is expressing social protest views. Examples of social protest are as follows:

Over 300 dead, we still got pride
We've lost all our morals, we still got pride
Should we fight this war in some far corner of the globe
And learn how to die for some unjust cause

Is this our future?
Ashes are all that remain
It's easy when you got pride

How much pride does a dead soldier got?
His life so short, no chance to even start

The ones he left behind
The world he'll never see
But no one could deny that the soldier died with pride

Minutemen, "Just Another Soldier," from album *3-Way Tie (For Last)*.
Copyright Cesstone Music 1985.
Reprinted with permission of the publisher.

Punk rock band touring the USA
Stopping along the Amerikkkan highway
Pull into the truckstop cuz I gotta take a leak
Everybody staring like I'm some kinda freak
Fuck all this attention I think I'll try to sneak
Into the ladies' room without getting caught
What? I just gotta use the pot
I gotta show you what I got?

'Excuse me sir? Over by the stall,
Wrong bathroom. The men's room's down the hall.'

So I pulled up my shirt to show I'm the gender
But the looks you're giving me are anything but tender
What's your problem? I ain't got a member
Fine I'll go into the boys' room
But it really fucking stinks
What's with your aim boy? You trying to hit the tank?

Your tomcat spray ferments so rank
So for you a little present
bloody tampon on the sink

Yeah my hair's pink I'm the missing link
You don't have a missing link bathroom

'Is that a he or a she?
Is that a him or a her?
Oh excuse me, ma'am…uh sir?'
Am I supposed to feel ashamed
Cuz you're confused
Cuz I don't fit into your box
You loser

'Excuse me ma'am your titties are kinda small
I'm still confused…'

Poor tired pathetic little sheep
Trying to limit me
With your dyke-otomies
Simple minds know two kinds
And I'm number three
You and Rush don't know shit about me
So let me pee
And gimme my free
Condiments in every bathroom

Tribe 8, "Wrong Bathroom," from album *Snarkism.*
Copyright Alternative Tentacles 1996.
Reprinted with permission of the publisher.

2. The operational definition for antiracism was based on Okolo's definition obtained from *Racism—A Philosophic Probe* (1974). Conceptually, antiracism is the rejection of the

> 'Mental or psychological attitude,' 'outlook,' 'mood,' or 'temper'…that regards one race (usually one's own) as essentially superior to another, often, on the basis of skin color or cultural achievement…[Or, antiracism can be defined as the rejection of a] preconceived judgment, view, or opinion of individuals or groups of one race concerning the members of another, often, usually on the basis of color…mode of dress, speech patterns, anatomical structures, or cultural achievements…[Regardless if

> it is] 'directed toward a group as a whole, or toward an individual because he [or she] is a member of that group' (pp. 6–7).

The singer is expressing antiracist views. Examples of antiracism are as follows:

> No matter what color, we're all guilty of prejudice…we better realize our differences…there's nothing wrong with pride of heritage—just remember your kind is not the only one…turn the fire down before the pot boils over
> Excerpt from Voodoo Glow Skulls, "Construction," *Firme*, Epitaph Records 1996.

> I'm moving up to Mendo
> Gonna raise some kids and not tell 'em 'bout Nintendo
> Just hope they don't grow up to be Nazi skins
> Cuz then I'll have to kill 'em and start over again
> Tra la le la
>
> I'm moving up to Mendo
> Livin' in my car that's what I intendo
> With my skateboard bungeed to the top
> I'll go anywhere cuz habitation's all a car is for
> Tra la le la
>
> I'm moving up to Mendo
> I'll panhandle 'til I can buy a pencil
> So I can write my memoirs but I won't have to rush
> It won't take long cuz I don't remember much
> Tra la.
>
> Tribe 8, "Mendo Hoo-Ha," from album *Snarkism*.
>

3. Antisexism was defined based on Lerner's (1986) definitions of sexism and patriarchy. The concept of antisexism/patriarchy is therefore the rejection of

> The manifestation and institutionalization of male dominance over women…in the family and the extension of male dominance over women in society in general. [Which]…implies that men [should not] hold power in all the important institutions of society and that women…[should not be]…deprived of access to such power…" (p. 239).

Therefore "the ideology of male supremacy, of male superiority and of beliefs that support and sustain it" (p. 240) are rejected here.

The singer is expressing antisexist views. Examples of antisexism are as follows.

Laugh you asshole and try to be brave
My God, what a strange shape
Drooling jaws are my dreams landscape
I am so tough and so afraid
Give it up, get it up, give it up, get it up
With spear, sword and blade
With spear, sword and blade

Hunt the She Beast
Mama bear is there beware
Hunt the She Beast

We got together because it was so fucking cold
And we knew the answer wasn't in the stars or in the soil
It was in blood
In a bloody run down to the sea, In a bloody run down to the sea
In a run down to the sun and sea
Hunt the She Beast
She bear, she bears the furies
Hunt the She Beast

Now I own everything and I have all the answers
Kingdom come like my father before and my son after
And it's power that brought me here
Brains and power and the fear
That fear that you've got to control
You've got to keep the women down below
That fear that you've got to control
You've got to keep the women down below
Cause there was something here before
The fear you've got to control
There is something down in that hole

Hunt the She Beast
Mama bear is there beware
Hunt the She Beast

And now there's nothing left to kill

You've bent the whole world to your will
When you reach out your mighty hand
There's nothing left but barren sand
you run and run and run
But you've forgotten what you're running from
You're flying into emptiness
And all that's left is emptiness
And all that's left for you is death
Now we don't need no prophets of doom
We need prophets of the womb
Deny your cruel mythology
Your fear inspired symbology
The circling arms of mother night
Will cradle your small firelight
From now on when I hunt to see
she
What do I see?
From now on when I hunt to see
she
What do I see?
A single
simple
human
being

Hunt the She Beast
She bear, she bears the future
Hunt the she beast

NOMEANSNO, "Hunt the She Beast," from album *Sex Mad.*
Copyright Alternative Tentacles 1987.
Reprinted with permission of the publisher.

4. The operational definition for the rejection of romantic love was based on the work of Mohan and Malone (1994).

> [I]ncludes references to [the rejection of] feelings of love, hearts, heartbreak…and any general statements about being in a romantic relationship or marriage (p. 298).

The singer is expressing anti-love/romantic views. Examples of anti-love/romantic views are as follows:

…My baby he's gone and I'm

Goin' too
My baby he's up in that house
In the sky
Cuz I shot him dead with no
Tear in my eye…
Excerpt from Red Ants, "Goin' Downtown," *Salt Box*, Epitaph Records 1996.

5. The conceptual definition for homosexual content was based on the work of Fenster (1992). It is expected that many songs will manifest references to homosexuality. Examples of such references include "…the possibilities and pleasures of homosexuals in" (Fenster 1992, 173) punk rock, frustration or disapproval with homophobic punk rockers, frustration with the lack of a local queer punk scene, problems with mainstream gay politics, frustration or disapproval with antigay legislation, and so forth.

The singer is expressing homosexuality in a positive light. Examples of positive homosexual themes are as follows:

struttin' on an i-beam in her steel toes and tool belt
tellin' all the boys what to do
takes off her hardhat
runs her hand through her crewcut
but don't let all those muscles fool you
she's a walkin' paradox in her jeans and her docs
sportin' big ugly tattoos
she goes home throws her legs in the air
hopin' no one heard the news

she's butch in the streets femme in the sheets
she's just a girl when she gets home
she wants to get plowed just like anyone else
don't let her fool you she's femme to the bone
butch in the streets femme in the sheets
butch in the streets femme in the sheets
butch in the streets femme in the sheets

walking' down the street in her leather at night
you like the way she mounts that harley-davidson bike
jump on the back
she gives it a rev
don't think she's gonna top you cuz she's belly up in bed
she's butch in the streets
femme in the sheets

> she's just a girl when she gets home
> she wants to get plowed like anyone else
> don't let her fool you she's femme to the bone
> butch in the streets femme in the sheets...
>
> Tribe 8, "Butch in the Streets," from album *Fist City*.
> Copyright Alternative Tentacles 1995.
> Reprinted with permission of the publisher.

6. The conceptual definition for the rejection of social protest was based on the work of Cole (1971). Antisocial protest: It is expected that punk songs will manifest few references to antisocial protest—defined as:

> ...Approval of situations existing in society or of attitudes widely held or [dis]approval of attitudes not held widely...presenting the 'system' (i.e. local or federal governments) in a favorable light, opposing revolution by presenting an unfavorable image of it, etc (p. 391).

The singer is expressing views against social protest. Examples are as follows:

> people are always thinking too much...we're not the ones—that want to change you or make you think—we're not the ones—to pressure you to change your ways—you go to school six hours a day—you got a job that doesn't pay—go out Friday night—you don't expect a lecture tonight...Excerpt from Voodoo Glow Skulls, "Method to This Madness," *Firme*, Epitaph Records 1996.

7. The operational definition for racism was based on Okolo's definition obtained from *Racism—A Philosophic Probe* (1974). Conceptually, racism, according to Okolo (1974), is:

> A 'mental or psychological attitude,' 'outlook,' 'mood,' or 'temper'...that regards one race (usually one's own) as essentially superior to another, often, on the basis of skin color or cultural achievement...[Or, racism can be defined as a prejudice as a] preconceived judgment, view, or opinion of individuals or groups of one race concerning the members of another, often, usually on the basis of color. Other factors, however, such as mode of dress, speech patterns, anatomical structures, or cultural achievements, are by no means excluded...'It may be directed toward a group as a whole, or toward an individual because he [or she] is a member of that group' (pp. 6–7).

The singer is expressing racist views. An example of a racist song is as follows:

> ...They all look so good just like my t.v. said they would but I'd trade them all for the ivory girl her skin is soft and white as snow not an ounce of tan green eyes and a mod haircut...Excerpt from Down by Law, "Ivory Girl," *All Scratched Up*, Epitaph Records 1996.

8. The operational definition for sexism was based on the work of Lerner (1986). According to Lerner (1986): "sexism and patriarchy mutually reinforce one another" (p. 240). Lerner defines the concept of patriarchy as:

> The manifestation and institutionalization of male dominance over women...in the family and the extension of male dominance over women in society in general. It implies that men hold power in all the important institutions of society and that women are deprived of access to such power. It does not imply that women are either totally powerless or totally deprived of rights, influence, and resources (p. 239).

Lerner (1986) defines the concept of sexism as "the ideology of male [or female] supremacy, of male [or female] superiority and of beliefs that support and sustain it" (p. 240). Sexism, as suggested by Lerner, is the result of the system of patriarchy [or matriarchy]. Sexual domination over others will also serve as an indicator of sexism.

The singer is expressing sexist views. Examples of sexist songs are as follows:

> flippersnapper flipperfashion
> baggy pants and romper boots
> gets the girlies every time
> we get no action she's so cute
>
> flippersnapper flipperfashion
> celtic tats on her head
> and a few in some other places
> seen by those she gets in bed
> flippersnapper
> she's so goddamn dapper
> all her girlfriends think she's fine
> last time we checked she had nine
> it's not fair
> let's all cut our hair like hers
> we don't care about individuality
> we want popularity and loads of promiscuity
>
> she had a million babes

then along came chloe
who said, 'I'm the only one'
and told 'em all 'blow me'

flippersnapper flipperfashion
flannel boxers, red bandanna
dressed like her and look what i got
anna anna anna anna

flippersnapper flipperfashion
white t-shirts and sleeveless flannels
sometimes she plays guitar
from her ringed lip dangles a camel

it's not fair
let's all cut our hair like hers
we don't care about individuality
we want popularity and loads of promiscuity

senior snacker
fashion leader
tell us where you shop, oh please
so we can get girlies and eat 'em too
jean-pierre flipper

so debonair
mr. flapper what you got there
pair o' boots you stole from na-na's?
t-shirt that downplays your ta-tas?
don't waste dough on strings and wah-wahs
jean-pierre you're the one
you just want to wear what's fun.

Tribe 8, "Flippersnapper," from album *Fist City*.

9. Love/Romance: The operational definition for this category was taken from Mohan and Malone (1994). Certain phrases referring to song titles and other categories not relevant to this study were omitted.

> Includes references to feelings of love, hearts, heartbreak, the use of words 'baby' or 'honey'...and any general statements about being in a romantic relationship or

> marriage. In general, if the word 'love' appears…the song will be coded in this category (p. 298).

The singer is expressing love/romantic views. Examples of love/romantic songs are as follows.

> …baby, I don't want you to come to me as a whore. Don't lust off my body baby, that's a bore. I see our love as being sacred, just you and me…maybe jah will bless us to be one tomorrow…Excerpt from Bad Brains, "Sacred Love," *I against I*, Bad Brains Publishing 1985.

10. The conceptual definition for homophobic songs was based on the work of Fenster (1992). Therefore, it is expected that many punk songs will contain homophobic content. Songs that express disapproval of homosexuality, advocate violence toward homosexuals, the use of language with the intent to harm, as in using the words faggot, homo, etc., or any negative references to homosexuals. Derogatory language, however, must not be taken out of context, for example, many homosexual punks self-identify as queer, faggot, etc., and therefore the same language when co-opted by homosexuals is not harmful but empowering.

Examples of homophobic songs are as follows:

> Had too many cold ones…because i'm scamming on a girl—who looks like a guy—just give me another drink—it'll make my day, and give me satisfaction…
> Excerpt from Voodoo Glow Skulls, "Trouble Walking," *Firme*, Epitaph Records 1996.

11. Absent: It is assumed that there will be lots of other messages in the coded lyrics. However, the "absent" category here is *only* for songs that do *not* fit into any of the ten categories mentioned above. The only songs to be coded as absent are those songs that have been coded as absent in all of the preceding ten categories.

The singer has not expressed any of the preceding views. Examples of songs to be classified as absent are as follows:

> …Lose your mind on a train. Take a ride. Excerpt from Red Aunts, "Bullet Train," *Salt Box*, Epitaph Records 1996.

Sampling

Based on Cole's work (1971) the unit of analysis for this study is song rather than line or word "because the overall message of each of the lyrics was considered the crucial factor" (p. 399). Thus, we composed a list of punk songs from which a sample could be drawn. After searching the World Wide Web, phoning music libraries, record stores, radio stations, and punk rock music producers, we concluded that there are no complete discographies of punk rock music available. The most significant factor that explains why there are no inclusive punk discographies has to do with the very nature of punk. Most punk bands do not stay together for long and many labels that record punk music also are relatively short-lived. Furthermore, many of the small labels punk bands sign with only print a few hundred copies of most songs before they are out of print or they disband. Because there are no complete discographies of punk from which a sample could be drawn, the releases of three record labels were used to compose a population. Thus the question arises: How do we know we developed a valid list of punk that most closely represents the most significant punk available in the United States since the late 1970s and early 1980s? In other words, why were labels used to create a list rather than some other source, and why did we choose the labels that were chosen?

One of the most readily available resources outlining significant punk music is the scholarly literature referenced throughout this book. However, because many of the bands and labels scholars have identified as important either no longer exist, are out of print or are not really punk, other sources were utilized. To obtain a sample of real punk, we decided to rely on the music identified as important by punk record store owners, punkers themselves, the punk rock producers Curry Malott interviewed, and Curry Malott himself. What we found was that most punk bands deemed important and significant in the United States appear on a few independent record labels, and that those labels themselves were considered to have had and continue to have significant roles in the distribution of the most relevant punk music. The population for this study is therefore comprised of all the albums and thus songs that appear on selected record labels. Everyone Curry Malott interviewed noted that there are and have been literally hundreds of punk labels, but there are a few labels that have and continue to produce the best, most relevant, influential punk, which are the labels that comprise the population for this study. For Malott himself, the Dead Kennedys, and Alternative Tentacles in general, were pivotal; they opened up a whole new way of looking at the world, a way to name the world for what it was and is, a white-supremacist, capitalist society that maintains itself through violence and deception.

It should be noted that not all of the labels in our population have every recording they have produced currently available. However, the sales representatives Malott talked with on the phone said that the lists are almost totally complete and do include the most important bands they have ever produced. The labels included in our sample are Alternative Tentacles (1), SST (2), and Epitaph (3). The claim is not being made that this list is representative of all punk throughout the 1980s and 1990s in the United States. Smaller, less influential labels exist that specialize in producing very specific messages, such as queer punk, which if included would have changed the results (i.e., larger percent of homosexual content). Other small punk labels exist that specialize in producing racist (and sexist) material, such as Resistance Records, that, if included, would also have altered the results. This study therefore does not represent all punk throughout the 1980s and 1990s. It is, however, representative of the three chosen labels, which we are arguing have been the most influential. At best, the results of this study reflect general trends in radical lefty punk rock throughout the 1980s and 1990s.

The first step in creating our three-label list (population) was to obtain label discographies from the labels, typically referred to as mail order catalogs, which are inclusive lists of albums particular labels have produced. The population parameters, album publication dates, number of songs on each album, sex and race/ethnicity of primary or lead singer, were found by utilizing various resources. These sources included each label's Web site if available, punk band Web sites created by independent individuals, personal contacts, looking on the actual records at record stores, and directly calling labels. Once the parameters of the population were obtained, a database was constructed on Microsoft Excel. Every song is represented by a row. Within each row, cell A represents band name and album; cell B represents label number, Alternative Tentacles (1), SST (2), and Epitaph (3); cell C represents song number; cell D represents publication date; cell E represents sex, male (0) and female (1); and, cell F represents race/ethnicity, coded as either white (0) or nonwhite (1). For example, row one represents song one from the album *Suffer* by the band Bad Religion. Row two represents song two from the album *Suffer* by the band Bad Religion, and so forth.

The list was stratified by decade, sex, race/ethnicity in order to eliminate sampling error on these variables (Babbie 1995). Consequently, six separate population lists were created:

- white females from the 1980s
- nonwhite males from the 1980s
- white males from the 1980s

- white females from the 1990s
- nonwhite males from the 1990s
- white males from the 1990s

The only female representation (singers) throughout the 1980s and 1990s were white. To obtain sufficient numbers of cases, disproportionate random samples of 51 cases were drawn from each of the six stratified sublists (with the exception of white females in the 1980s with 36 cases). A random numbers table was employed to draw the samples (Babbie 1995). The sample size (291) was based on probability sampling theory, which holds that the larger the sample size, the less sampling error (Babbie 1995), and the available time for coding. When it was not possible to locate lyrics for a song, additional songs were sampled as needed.

Coding

The sample of 291 songs was coded by hand, but before coding we had to check the operational definitions for reliability, which was done by double-coding songs. Sharpening, or fine-tuning the operational definitions is the object of double-coding, which, if successful, increases reliability. Double-coding means that two people code the same set of songs and then compare and contrast their results (Miles & Huberman 1984). Curry Malott and an individual unfamiliar with this study separately coded two different sets of songs, two weeks apart. However, the individual who assisted in the double-coding is a self-identified white, male, feminist, radical, punker.

It was assumed that if the coding system were reliable, then the two people coding would code songs the same way. On the first pretest, we did not "expect better than 70% intercoder reliability, using the formula: "reliability = number of agreements/total number of agreements plus disagreements" (Miles & Huberman 1984, 63). Especially when coding latent content, text is subject to individual interpretation. However, an overall intercoder reliability of 88.55% was achieved on the first pretest coding 27 songs. The major source of disagreement was what constituted sexist and antisexist content for female singers. Even though the conceptual definition of sexism included women as capable of sexism (internalized oppression), and a song by a woman was used to operationally define sexism, the second coder was still uneasy about coding messages perpetuated by women as sexist given women's marginalized status in U.S. society. Through dialogue we agreed that some women employing the punk aesthetic do perpetuate sexist ideology, usually in the form of women sexually dominating other women—a form of internalized oppression. In this case, the oppressed individuals who are dehumanized because of their oppression strive to become more human, but because of distorted ideas of what it means to be human, they take on the role of oppressor believing that to be human means to be an oppressor (Freire 1970b). Similarly, some women expressed sexual domination over men, therefore continuing to promote sexism through sexual domination.

The second pretest, two weeks later, was comprised of 18 new songs and resulted in a 96% overall intercoder reliability, a 7.45% increase from the first pretest. The majority of disagreements were in the category love/romance, but proved to be only minor disagreements resulting from slight subjective differences in song interpretation. Double coding did, therefore, serve to more precisely determine how text was to be interpreted.

Chapter 7

Results: What We Learned from Doing a Content Analysis

The purpose of this section is to present the results of the content analysis. The content analysis, the quantitative aspect of this book, is an attempt to shed light on the intricate interconnectedness of norms and values of six subgroups of punk and dominant society, and also to highlight general message trends over time. These findings therefore emerged as a complex web of articulations, representations, and contradictions, at the same time both accommodative and resistive to the dominant culture in the United States. We attempt to paint as complete a picture of this web as possible paying particular attention to unravel and distort it as little as possible. In the next section we attempt to introduce some qualitative elements into this largely quantitative project. The qualitative aspect, the thick description of artists and analysis of individual songs, is also an attempt to highlight important differences and similarities within and among groups. Punk rockers in the United States comprise a heterogeneous group with often-disparate political orientations and worldviews varying from and within particular time periods. We therefore do not intend to generalize our findings to the entire population of punk rockers at any point in time. What follows are the results from the content analysis part of this project.

A blank code form was used as a template to guide the creation of the database on the spreadsheet computer program Microsoft Excel. The database created on Excel was saved as a file compatible with a more advanced computer program, SPSS (Statistical Package for the Social Sciences of SPSS, Incorporated), where the statistics were run. Date the song was produced, race/ ethnicity of singer, and sex of singer served as independent variables, which are all nominal level data. The ten categories that comprise old and new values, plus the category "absent" comprise the dependent variables, which are also nominal level. The first findings, however, were the percentages of white males, nonwhite males, and females from 1980 to 1997 as message presenters.

The creation of the population parameters discussed in the sampling section allowed us to look at and analyze how many white male, white female, and nonwhite male singers there were in the 1980s and 1990s thus far (see Table 7.0). We were able to identify 1,572 noninstrumental songs produced in the 1980s (see Table 7.1). Ninety-two percent (1,451) of those songs were sung by white males; 4.5% (68) were sung by nonwhite males, African Americans, and Latinos; and the remaining 3.5% (53) were sung by white females. We were able to identify 2,314 noninstrumental songs produced in the 1990s (see Table 7.1). Eighty percent (1,855) of those songs were sung by white males, a decrease of 12% since the 1980s. Fourteen percent (313) of those songs were sung by nonwhite males, an increase of 9.5%, which included African Americans, Latinos, and one Japanese band on Alternative Tentacles, Ultra Bide. The remaining 6% (146) were sung by white females, an increase of 2.5% since the 1980s. When the two decades are combined (3,886 noninstrumental songs), 5% (199) of the songs were sung by white women, 10% (381) were sung by nonwhite men, and 85% (3,306) were sung by white men. As expected, the percentage of women and nonwhites as message presenters increased substantially, but what messages have these artists been perpetuating?

Table 7.0. Population Breakdown

1980s	1990s	Total
1,572	2,314	3,886

Table 7.1. Sex/Race Breakdown

	White Males	Nonwhite Males	White Females	Total
1980s	92% (1,451)	4.5% (68)	3.5% (53)	1,572
1990s	80% (1,855)	14% (313)	6% (146)	2,314
Total	85% (3,306)	10% (381)	5% (199)	3,886

Simple frequency distributions were run to show percentages of message trends over time (see Table 7.2). Because we analyzed each subpopulation separately and comparatively, we did not need to worry about differential sampling at this point (Babbie 1995). As expected, the dominant theme from the 1980s to the present was social protest. Every subgroup from the 1980s to the 1990s were coded as containing 76% social protest with the exception of white females from the 1980s, of which 50% were coded as containing social protest. Unexpectedly, however, most groups contained very little sexism. The largest amount of sexism (25%) was found in the white female group from the 1990s. Twenty-nine percent of the songs sung by white females in the 1990s contained homosexual content. In coding, many of the songs white females sung in the 1990s coded as sexist were also coded as containing homosexual content—women dominating women. As expected, nonwhite males in both the 1980s and 1990s had the highest frequency of antiracism, although the amount of antiracist content did decrease markedly (16%) from the 1980s to the 1990s for nonwhite males while increasing slightly for all other groups. A dominant theme in the 1980s was love/romance, which, as expected, decreased significantly in the 1990s. One of the most interesting results was in the category "Absent." Twenty-eight percent of the songs by white females in the 1980s did not contain content in any of the ten remaining categories. Could this be revealing our own biases and the male bias of past researchers used to guide this study? We address this question in Chapter 8 (p. 98).

Table 7.2. Value Content in Percentages and Raw Numbers

	White Males 1980s	White Males 1990s	Nonwhite Males 1980s	Nonwhite Males 1990s	White Females 1980s	White Females 1990s
	(n = 51)	(n = 51)	(n = 51)	(n = 51)	(n = 36)	(n = 51)
Social Protest	76% (39)	76% (39)	76% (39)	76% (39)	50% (18)	76% (39)
Antiracist	8% (4)	10% (5)	43% (22)	27% (14)	6% (2)	12% (6)
Antisexist	2% (1)	6% (3)	10% (5)	4% (2)	11% (4)	12% (6)
Anti-love/ Romance	12% (6)	4% (2)	2% (1)	2% (1)	11% (4)	22% (11)
Homosexual	0%	2% (1)	0%	0%	6% (2)	29% (15)
Antisocial Protest	0%	0%	0%	0%	0%	0%
Racist	0%	2% (1)	0%	0%	0%	0%
Sexist	14% (7)	14% (7)	20% (10)	6% (3)	11% (4)	25% (13)
Love/ Romance	14% (7)	14% (7)	27% (14)	8% (4)	22% (8)	14% (7)
Homophobic	2% (1)	0%	2% (1)	0%	0%	0%
Absent	8% (4)	12% (6)	6% (3)	16% (8)	28% (10)	4% (2)

As a summary of the value content in percentages and raw numbers, the number of songs (51 and 36) in each subgroup containing resistant messages and accommodating messages were totaled (see Table 7.3). Recall that social protest, antiracist, antisexist, anti-love/romance, and homosexual were coded as indicators of resistance. Antisocial protest, racist, sexist, love/romance, and homophobic were coded as indicators of accommodation. In addition, the number of resistant messages and the number of accommodating messages for each subgroup were also computed (see Table 7.4). The number of cases in Table 7.3 represents the *number of songs* in each category (51 and 36). The number of cases in Table 7.4 represents the *number of messages*, which is the number of songs multiplied by the number of categories (10) or 510 and 360.

In sum, resistance has been prevalent for all six subgroups and accommodation was low (see Table 7.3). The most counts of resistance were perpetuated by white women in the 1990s (see Table 7.4). The most counts of accommodation were perpetuated by nonwhite males in the 1980s (see Table 7.4). Pearson's R® was used to determine the statistical significance of the findings thus far.

Table 7.3. Number of Songs with Resistant and Accommodative Messages per Subgroup

	White Males 1980s	White Males 1990s	Nonwhite Males 1980s	Nonwhite Males 1990s	White Females 1980s	White Females 1990s
	(n = 51)	(n = 51)	(n = 51)	(n = 51)	(n = 36)	(n = 51)
Resistant	80% (41)	76% (39)	76% (39)	76% (39)	53% (19)	86% (44)
Accommodative	24% (12)	22%(11)	37% (19)	14% (7)	28% (10)	37% (19)

Table 7.4. Number of Resistant and Accommodative Messages per Subgroup

	White Males 1980s	White Males 1990s	Nonwhite Males 1980s	Nonwhite Males 1990s	White Females 1980s	White Females 1990s
	(n = 510)	(n = 510)	(n = 510)	(n = 510)	(n = 360)	(n = 510)
Resistant	10% (50)	10% (50)	13% (67)	11% (56)	9% (30)	15% (77)
Accommodative	3% (15)	3% (15)	5% (25)	1% (7)	3% (12)	4% (20)

R was computed on SPSS to determine the statistical relationship between variables. We were able to use r, a normed measure of association, because all the variables are scored as either present (1) or absent (0) and can therefore be treated as interval level. The categories of social protest and absent had the overall highest correlations among all six subgroups (see Table 7.5). What follows is a summary of the findings ® by subgroup: white males 1980s and white males 1990s; nonwhite males 1980s and nonwhite males 1990s; and white females 1980s and white females 1990s, respectively. Note that only correlations that are statistically significant at the .05 level are provided in Table 7.5.

As expected, there was a strong negative relationship for white male singers in the 1980s between social protest and love/romance, r = –.450, which increased slightly in the 1990s, r = –.553. In other words, songs that were protesting society were highly unlikely to also perpetuate an affirmation of dominant conceptions of love/romance. It was expected that sexist content would be high for white males, but it wasn't; it was only 14% for white males in the 1980s and 1990s. It is therefore not surprising that sexism was not highly correlated with any other variable. Contrary to what was expected, there was a moderate, positive relationship between sexist and homosexual in the 1990s, r = .355, which did not exist during the 1980s. Finally, there was a strong negative relationship between social protest and absent in the 1990s, r = .658, which in the 1980s was r = .526. Because social protest was so high in both the 1980s and 1990s (76%), it is not surprising that there was such a strong negative relationship between social protest and absent. In other words, if a song did not contain social protest, it probably did not contain anything we were looking for.

Nonwhite males were also high in social protest (76%), but differed from their white counterparts in significant ways. Nonwhite males in the 1980s were coded the highest in antiracist content (43%), 36% more than the next highest group, white males. Therefore, it is not surprising that there was a moderate relationship between social protest and antiracist, r = +.483, which decreased in the 1990s to r = +.341. There was a moderate, negative relationship between antiracist and sexist unique to the 1980s, r = .330. There was a moderate, negative relationship between sexist and social protest in the 1980s, r = .425. This relationship was statistically insignificant in the 1990s. The negative relationship between love and social protest deceased from moderate in the 1980s, r = .487, to statistically insignificant in the 1990s. There was a statistically significant relationship between love and antisexist in the 1990s, r = +.317, which did not exist in the 1980s or in any other subgroup. Finally, the negative, moderate relationship between social protest and absent in the 1980s, r = –.451, increased to a strong negative relationship in the 1990s, r = –.778.

White women varied from and were similar to both themselves and white and nonwhite men in both the 1980s and 1990s (see Table 7.5). For white women in the 1980s, the relationship between social protest and antisexist became statistically insignificant in the 1990s, but was statistically significant in the 1980s, r = +.354 (see Table 7.5). The relationship between social protest and sexist was moderate, increasing from r = –.354 in the 1980s to r = –.418 in the 1990s. There was also a moderate, positive relationship between love/romance and homosexual unique to the 1980s, r = +.454. There was also a weak relationship between absent and love/romance unique to the 1980s, r = –.332. Like every other subgroup, there was a negative relationship between social protest and absent. The relationship, however, went from strong, r = –.620, in the 1980s to moderate, r = –.364, in the 1990s. What follows is a more in-depth analysis of the findings and implications.

Table 7.5. Correlations Statistically Significant at the .05 Level

	White Males 1980s	White Males 1990s	Nonwhite Males 1980s	Nonwhite Males 1990s	White Females 1980s	White Females 1990s
Social Protest/ Love	–.450	–.553	–.487			
Social Protest/ Sexist			–.425		–.354	–.418
Social Protest/ Antisexist					+.354	
Social Protest/ Antiracist			+.483	+.341		
Sexist/ Homosexual		+.355				
Sexist/ Antiracist			–.330			
Love/ Homosexual					+.454	
Love/ Antisexist				+.317		
Absent/ Love					–.332	
Absent/ Social Protest	–.526	–.658	–.451	–.778	–.620	–.364

Chapter 8

Discussion: Putting It All Together

The following discussion of songs by decade with thick descriptions of artists is used to paint a picture of the 1980s and 1990s highlighting what we think are dominant aspects of the two decades and of the results of this study. In other words, we look at what events and figures shaped the decades and what the punk rockers on the three labels were trying to say as well as do through their music during these periods. We are particularly interested in looking at the resistant aspects that might be deemed threatening to mainstream, transnational corporate interests, and accommodative aspects that in our opinion support mainstream, transnational corporate interests, and the many disparities within and between, and how they have changed over time. To do so, we theoretically situate our discussion and punk rockers in a social, historical context paying particular attention to how we are all implicated in a hegemonic structure that dehumanizes everyone involved (Freire 1970b), which is the object of our critiques.

Like society at large, punk rockers do not comprise a static, cohesive, or homogeneous group of individuals. The dominant view of reality, the ontology, is that some people are intellectually and morally superior and some intellectually and morally inferior, thus legitimating the unequal distributions of power and wealth within U.S. society. Punk rockers have not been immune to this view of reality, and thus often situate themselves in the position of intellectual and moral superior over those or that which is in question, quite often each other. In fact, according to Biafra (1994), occupants of alternative cultural spaces, punk rockers in particular, are far too preoccupied with fighting each other over issues of authenticity, hindering the struggle for humanization in general and the possibility of massive, systematic, social revolution in particular. According to Arlene Stein (1997),

> All identity-based movements have a tendency to fall into what Alberto Melucci has termed 'integralism,' the yearning for a totalizing identity, for a 'master key which unlocks every door of reality.' Integralism, says Melucci, rejects a pluralist and

> 'disenchanted' attitude to life and encourages people to 'turn their backs on complexity' and become incapable of recognizing difference (p. 386).

While we are not arguing that punk rock constitutes a social movement, it is nonetheless part of the struggle for justice and humanization. It is a counterculture that has traditionally been based largely on identity, and as Biafra alluded, has been guilty of "integralism," white supremacy in particular, as we suggested earlier.

Therefore, in an effort to maintain and expand on avenues for noncorporate-controlled perspectives, it would be far more productive for more punkers to collectively begin to push themselves in weeding out the values, ideas, and beliefs of the dominant society that we and they have all internalized. Reflecting on and critiquing that which we internalize is what can lead to new social action and ultimately social change. We argue that what many punkers have done is to start with small actions, mainly engaging discourse, often to say more about themselves than those or that which we and they are critiquing. This is at the heart of what ultimately happens in identity formations and the political alignments and realignments in identity politics. Ultimately, these acts of social protest are about creating collectives to fight the social enemies and institutions that are designed to quite literally destroy not only alternative cultural spaces, but people, humanity, and life in general.

In a talk on censorship, Biafra (1994) discussed the roles played by Tipper Gore and various other political figures like Bill Clinton, the PMRC (Parents Music Resource Center), Wal-Mart, Blockbuster Video, and the Christian Right in general, in putting alternative record companies out of business. They are seen as part of an effort to further homogenize mass media and the entertainment industry, in short, to limit the range of political perspectives available to consumers. For example, Tipper Gore and the PMRC would like to pass a federal law requiring companies to put "parental advisory stickers" on all records with "explicit" lyrics, which according to Biafra (1994), would "steamroll or bulldoze" much of the independent music scene. According to Biafra (1994), Susan Baker of the PMRC said in one of Biafra's (1994) songs on censorship, "we have to go after the independents." It is the independents, in particular, we argue, that often reveal the social injustices that make the dominant power structure look bad, a point we later return to. From our perspective, it is the independents that could potentially mobilize youth, unsupervised by parental control, in ways that scare the status quo.

As of the early 1990s, between eight and 12 multinational corporations controlled 80% of all mass media, television, newspapers, radio, movies, and music—in other words, everything (Biafra 1994; Chomsky & Herman 1988). If successful, the only mass media perspectives influencing the way we see and react to the world would be that of multinational corporations and other interest groups vested in society's norms and values (Biafra 1994; Chomsky & Herman 1988). In such a world, every perspective in popular culture that might call into question multinational corporate interests or challenge the status quo, whether in support of working people, women, people of color, the environment, and so forth, would be silenced. The labels and the artists on their records analyzed in this study would be silenced. With George W. Bush as president we are in for more of the same censorship and attack against the type of challenges brought by nonconformist beliefs expressed by punks and other alternative thinkers.

The punk rock labels we analyzed, however, have become more inclusive. This is potentially more threatening to corporate interests. The 1999 World Trade Organization (WTO) rebellions in Seattle, Washington, where over 50,000 environmentalists, urban organizers, and labor organizers from all over the world represented the growing international labor movement protested what to many is an increasingly global capitalist order. The new economic order has brought us to a point in human history where globally there are more people living in poverty than at any other point in human history, which has been made possible through free trade agreements like NAFTA (North American Free Trade Agreement) and GATT (General Agreement on Tariffs and Trade) (Kloby 1999; McMichael 2000). As politicians like George W. Bush and Al Gore spoke of the growth and prosperity of the U.S. economy, punk rock played and continues to play to expose them and people like them.

In this context of conservative, global, economic greed promoted by wealth and privilege, there are still those who are preoccupied with fixing boundaries and making punk label membership more exclusive, as noted by Biafra (1994). In an effort to break down punk rock exclusiveness, Biafra has incorporated many voices and perspectives into his label, Alternative Tentacles. Biafra, himself a punk rocker, supports an entire label of relatively like-minded occupants of this alternative cultural space who are fundamentally opposed to the norms and values of dominant U.S. society. Others labels include SST, which seems to have become more inclusive since the 1980s. Epitaph, though more palatable to mainstream interests and more homogeneous than the other two labels, nonetheless assumes a slightly different approach to the struggle.

As previously stated, punk rock emerged out of a general disapproval of and boredom with dominant society (Biafra 1994; Dancis 1978; Laing 1985). Punk rock therefore is a tactic that subverts and resists, although never quite able to completely resist, every oppressive aspect of dominant society. Punk rock emerged as and continues to be a new and exciting form of political expression in a time of increasing state-enforced censorship of alternative perspectives.

Some punk rockers and the spaces they create and maintain, such as Biafra, have retained experimental qualities. Consequently, punk rock can no longer be characterized the way it was characterized in the late 1970s and 1980s by scholars such as Dixon et al. (1979) and Dancis (1978) who labeled punk as loud, repetitive, simple, angry, white, male, and against society. While punk is undoubtedly still all of those things, as we demonstrate, it has become much more than that. Thus, punk rock is fluid and historically contingent, best characterized as a cultural space rather than as a musical style. It is no longer just one style, but a place—one of the only places—where groups and individuals with varying styles can express ideas and tell stories that would not be heard otherwise. Original punk rock styles of the late 1970s, 1980s, and even some of the 1990s (i.e., the style of the group Nirvana), have been co-opted by the mainstream, and can be bought in "clean" versions at corporate chains like Wal-Mart and seen on MTV. New styles, such as those found in this study, like spoken word and music without identifiable rhythms or beats have limited availability and, according to Biafra (1994), tend not to be seen or heard in most record stores. Both new and old styles are found in varying forms and degrees in our content analysis.

As we suggested previously, punk and mainstream are not dichotomous but continuous. Alternative cultural spaces and those who occupy them, and mainstream cultural spaces and those who occupy them, are woven together by overlapping contradictory ideas and actions with extremism on both ends. Indeed, those reared in a "smoggy" (i.e., racist, capitalist) place cannot be free of the effects of that smog (Tatum 1997). Thus, in our efforts to create a more humane way of life there will no doubt surface traces of the old system, for unlearning and becoming is a lifelong process (Freire 1970b). According to Freire, revolution is made possible only through the love of humanity and human liberation. In an unloving, dehumanized society, it is love that we are deprived of, and which is needed to become more human, but in coming to that realization we must unlearn oppressive ideologies. Even punk rock has evolved despite the fact that there always existed a revolutionary potential in its social protest.

Social protest was the most dominant theme among all six subgroups in both the 1980s and 1990s (see Table 7.2, p. 91). Even so, there was a wide variety of aspects and issues that singers raised in their music and thus the music varied from the 1980s to the 1990s. Many of them reflected the diversity within their subgroups and society in general. Nonetheless, social protest, as the center of the complex web of articulations and contradictions, was intimately related to all of the other significant variables analyzed in our content analysis—love/romance, anti-love/romance, sexist, antisexist, antiracist, homosexual, and absent. These findings serve as the foundation for broader discussion of punk.

As discussed earlier, the Cold War, racist politics, and the breakdown of income redistribution during the 1980s agitated many late teenagers and twenty-year-olds like Jello Biafra, who had not forgotten the fight for and anticipated social equality of the 1960s and early 1970s. So, was the emergence of U.S. punk rock an extension of the 1960's social protest? What specifically was being protested? Specifically, what norms and values of dominant society were being contested or promoted by this later generation?

As previously noted, some of what singers were protesting in society coded as homosexuality, antisexist, anti-love/romance, and antiracist. Thus, our findings show that white women coded the highest in social protest issues relating to sex and gender (see Table 7.2, p. 91). Nonwhite males coded the highest on antiracist messages (see Table 7.2). Most of what white males protested coded as just social protest, but could also have been coded as antiwar, antigovernment, and/or anticapitalism. However, these are just generalizations, there was much overlap.

The Descendents, recorded on SST during the 1980s, were well known as "good" traditional California punk rock. Milo Aukerman, a white male, is the singer. The Descendents have a basic punk sound; a fast tempo, simple three-chord guitar riffs, shouted/sung vocals, and songs tend to last only a minute or two. The Descendents shortest song, "All" (1987), is one second. "All" has one chord played one time with only one word for vocals all yelled one time. When the Descendents play for longer than one second, they often protest society in such songs as "I Don't Want to Grow Up" (1987), and mainstream consumerism in "Rockstar" (1987). The Descendents, however, sang a lot of love songs in the 1980s, such as "Good Good Things" (1987), perpetuating dominant conceptions of male and female sexuality, which served to contradict their frequent anti-society themes. As Mumia Abu-Jamal notes in *All Things*

000), referring to love songs among African American recording artists:

> For a generation born into America's chilling waters of discontent, into the 1970s and '80s, into periods of denial, cutbacks, and emergent white supremacy, one must understand how love songs sound false and discordant, out of tune with their gritty, survivalist realities (p. 124).

Thus, as the superficiality of love songs holds true among African American artists, so too does it hold true among white artists such as the Descendants. However, most of the white male punkers in the 1980s on the three labels we analyzed did not record love songs, and very rarely addressed issues relating to love/romance.

An all-white male band from San Pedro, California, called the Minutemen, produced many albums on SST throughout much of the 1980s, none of which we coded as containing messages that support traditional conceptions of love/romance. The Minutemen most often protested war, capitalism, the U.S. government, and dominant society in general. Most of their songs are under a minute and are yelled, chanted, or talked rather than sung. For example, the following song, "Paranoid Chant," is characteristic of the Minutemen and much of early 1980s California-based white, male punk rock.

> i try to work and i keep thinking of world war three
> i try to talk to girls and i keep thinking of world war three
> the god damn six o'clock news makes sure i keep thinking of
> world war three
> i got a mile of numbers and a ton of stats
> of warheads
> of being shot in the forehead!!!
> i don't even worry about crime anymore
> so many god damned scared faces
> i keep thinking of russia, of russia!!!
> paranoid stuck on overdrive
> paranoid scared shitless
>
> Minutemen, "Paranoid Chant," from *Paranoid Time.*
>

In "Paranoid Chant," D. Boon clearly protests the mainstream U.S. media for its role in instilling the fear of nuclear war and Russia on the masses, including D. Boon himself.

Given D. Boon's commitment to radical politics, he was probably alluding to the Red Scare, and the social creation of an enemy justifying the increased governmental expenditure on the production of an enormously huge military complex (Zinn 1980; Melman 1970). However, this song is not free from all of the oppressive ideas of the dominant society. In the line, "i try to talk to girls and i keep thinking of world war three," D. Boon does not challenge male domination (i.e., sexism). Thus, for us, D. Boon maintains his position of domination over women by implying that he controls the discourse between himself and girls, and perhaps even that he can talk to other men about the threat of a third world war but not to women. What message does that send? Or, more specifically, what message is sent when what exists (sexism) is not challenged? That men are intellectually superior to women and therefore we need not question it? That women are merely just an "other"—a subordinate part of heterosexual relationships? What D. Boon provides is a simplified analysis of a complex issue, war and media, employing a fairly simplistic format of punk rock. But D. Boon fails to check his own white male heterosexism.

Another extremely influential band from the 1980s was the Dead Kennedys, headed by vocalist Jello Biafra, a white male. In the do-it-yourself spirit of punk rock Biafra, in 1979, with his own label Alternative Tentacles, released the Dead Kennedys first single, *California Über Alles*. Then, in 1985 the Dead Kennedys released *Frankenchrist*, which included a poster of *Penis Landscape* by the Swiss artist H. R. Giger. In 1986 Jello Biafra, the Dead Kennedys, and Alternative Tentacles were taken to court by the California judicial authorities for "Distributing Harmful Matter to Minors" (Biafra 1994)—*Penis Landscape*—and thus were the first in U.S. history to be taken to court over a music album. According to Biafra (1994), he was not on trial because he was selling *Penis Landscape* to minors, but because through their lyrics, concerts, and record label, the Dead Kennedys posed a threat to the state and capitalism in general by challenging the religious Right. Despite the temporary setback, the following song, "Holiday in Cambodia," has been referred to as the band's definitive moment, an important 1980's white male punk song. It was first released as a single in June 1980 and then appeared on *Fresh Fruit for Rotting Vegetables* in September 1980. However, because of a recent lawsuit against Jello Biafra and Alternative Tentacles for royalties and rights to Dead Kennedys' music by his former bandmates, Dead Kennedys' guitar player East Bay Ray in particular, "Holiday in Cambodia" appears courtesy of East Bay Ray and Decay Music. On his most recent and most important spoken-word album, *Become the Media* (2000), Biafra holds that this lawsuit is the result of his refusal to allow the jean manufacturer Levis to use "Holiday in Cambodia" in a commercial arguing that someone had to take a stand against unjust corporations using our favorite songs to sell products produced in the most inhumane of conditions.

So you've been to school for a year or two
And you know you've seen it all
In daddy's car thinkin' you'll go far
Back east your type don't crawl

Play ethnicky jazz to parade your snazz
On your five grand stereo
Braggin' that you know how the niggers feel the cold
And the slum's got so much soul
It's time to taste what you most fear
Right Guard will not help you here
Brace yourself, my dear
Brace yourself, my dear

It's a holiday in Cambodia
It's tough kid, but it's life
It's a holiday in Cambodia
Don't forget to pack a wife

You're a star-belly sneech you suck like a leach
You want everyone to act like you
Kiss ass while you bitch so you can get rich
But your boss gets richer off you
Well you'll work harder with a gun in your back
For a bowl of rice a day
Slave for soldiers 'till you starve
Then your head is skewered on a stake
Now you can go where people are one
Now you can go where they get things done
What you need, my son…
What you need, my son…

Is a holiday in Cambodia
Where people dress in black
A holiday in Cambodia
Where you'll kiss ass or crack

Pol Pot, Pol Pot, Pol Pot, Pol Pot, etc.
And it's a holiday in Cambodia

Where you'll do what you're told
A holiday in Cambodia
Where the slums got so much soul

Dead Kennedys, "Holiday in Cambodia," *Fresh Fruit for Rotting Vegetables.*
Reprinted with permission courtesy of Decay Music. Copyright 1980.

In "Holiday in Cambodia," Biafra, using his yuppie-baiting tactics, implicitly criticizes social inequality in the United States and what we consider a limited criticism of war.

By employing stereotypical, unsympathetic images of rich kids and recalcitrant leaders, Biafra detracts from the horrifying realities of war. The accompanying music, however, is evil sounding serving to maintain some of the depressing, unpleasant feelings war often engenders. The line "Don't forget to pack a wife" we interpreted as antisexist because of the sarcastic tone of the song. That line seems to be another jab at mainstream norms and values, but in this case the value of "owning" a wife.

Antiwar/social protest content was also prevalent among certain nonwhite male bands during the 1980s. San Francisco–based The Beatnigs, headed by African American activist Spearhead, protested war in a number of songs on their self-titled album The Beatnigs, released in 1988 on Alternative Tentacles, such as "CIA," "Control," and "Rooticus Sporaticus." Among these songs we found a moderate, positive relationship between social protest and antiracism ($r = +.483$) unique to nonwhite males in the 1980s. The Beatnigs' "Control" (1988) demonstrates their antiracism/social protest and antiwar themes prevalent during the 1980s.

Control
In South Africa today
Military sources reported
that the rioting in the homeland has increased
The system of Apartheid is slipping

In South Africa today
Military sources reported
that four miners were killed and twenty-one injured
in racially motivated violence

In South Africa today
Military sources reported

that a peaceful compromise could not be reached
after years of violence?

In South Africa today
military sources were sad to say
that the system of Apartheid
is finished!
But we must maintain control!
We must maintain control?
We must maintain control!

Freedom, freedom
Free yourself, freedom!
Freedom, freedom
Free yourself, freedom!

The Beatnigs, "Control," from album *The Beatnigs.*

The record this song appeared on, The Beatnigs (1988), comes with what the band calls an "Aural Instruction Manual," which is a black-and-white newsprint zine that centers the lyrics of each song in a collage of text and pictures, visually highlighting the dominant themes of each song—a format that Biafra has been using since at least 1980. The lyrics to "Control" are surrounded by what appear to be pictures of black South African revolutionaries and white military troops sporting full riot gear and toting big guns, further highlighting the song's social protest, antiracist and antigovernment stance. Some nonwhite male singers in the 1980s who protested racism but not war, focused on other issues.

Bad Brains, an African American high-speed reggae/punk band from Washington, DC, who recorded on SST during the 1980s, for example, protested racism in some songs while supporting traditional heterosexual relationships in others. Moreover, Bad Brains has been criticized for their homophobic content in queer punk zines, such as *Homocore* (Fenster 1992). We did not, however, code any of Bad Brains' songs as homophobic, nor have we heard any overtly homophobic songs by Bad Brains. However, we did code some of their songs as sexist and love/romance, accommodating dominant conceptions of sexuality. The following song, "Sacred Love," is from the 1986 release *I against I.*

> ...baby, i don't want you to come to me as a whore. don't lust off my body baby, that's a bore. i see our love as being sacred, just you and me...maybe jah will bless us to be one tomorrow...Excerpt from Bad Brains, "Sacred Love," *I against I*, Bad Brains Publishing 1985.

The voice in this song is an example of the assertive, dominating male-setting relationship and sexual boundaries and ways of being and not being for his prospective permanent partner.

"Sacred Love" could be interpreted as perpetuating male domination and female subordination, which seems contradictory to "Let Me Help," a song off the same album that praises equality. We guess when H. R. Throat, the singer, said "universal all live as one" in "Let Me Help" he was just referring to men. However, as is true with songs by women, being a white man in a white-supremacist society, perhaps there are more life-affirming messages in "Sacred Love" than we were able to detect. In "Let Me Help," however, we did detect messages we considered to be resistant to dominant society.

> economics legality (chuck it). does it show we love to be free...for tomorrow we generate the courage today. is your will about to quake and melt. let me help...psychopathic brutality (stop it)...universal all live as one...Excerpt from Bad Brains, "Let Me Help," *I against I*, Bad Brains Publishing 1985.

In "Let Me Help" we hear what Mumia Abu-Jamal in *All Things Censored* (2000) calls "the ancient African spirit of resistance, that stuff seeded in us by our ancestors" (p. 126), which we took to mean the life-affirming message of solidarity and of being in struggle against an unjust system with one's community and people.

Like nonwhite males, white women in the 1980s frequently focused on issues of sex and gender as well as social protest as themes for songs. Women sang very few songs of the type we analyzed in the 1980s—54 that we were able to identify. And though women in the 1980s had many correlates between variable pairs (see Table 7.5, p. 94), white women had the highest percentage of songs coded as absent (29%, see Table 7.2, p. 91). So what were white women in the 1980s singing about that we failed to anticipate? In 1988, L7 put out their first record on Epitaph called *L7*. Every song was coded, and most were coded as absent because we were uncertain of the messages they were perpetuating. "Bite the Wax Tadpole" is the first song on the album and was coded as absent. L7 plays a fairly standard version of punk, which sounds very heavy-metalish.

One of the songs on this record is even called "Metal Stampede." On various Web sites we looked at, the women in the band are portrayed like many male punkers, as beer-drinking, tough, hard-core ragers from Los Angeles.

> bite the wax, bite the wax tadpole
> bite it_tadpole...
> hide the hole
> hide the hole in your head, baby...
> Excerpt from L7, "Bite the Wax Tadpole," from album *L7*, Epitaph Records 1988.

The lyrics to "Bite the Wax Tadpole" were obtained from a Web site unconnected to the band or the label.

We assume the ellipses represent words the transcriber was unable to decipher. A "wax tadpole" could mean virtually anything, possibly a sperm? Consequently, the song could be a sexual innuendo. Tragic Mulatto is another female band who made records in the 1980s, but do not perpetuate the traditional male punk aesthetic. Many of Tragic Mulatto's songs on *Hot Man Pussy* released in 1989 on Alternative Tentacles were coded as absent because we couldn't understand the lyrics and were unable to find printed lyrics. However, we were able to find a short Tragic Mulatto biography in "Trouser Press," which is connected to "Music Boulevard," an online music store. In the biography, Ira Robbins describes them as occupants of a "bizarre musical universe" who often sarcastically sing about menstruation and how to have sex. Much of their music sounds like

> an ominous rock rumble with jagged horn noise and dramatic vocals. Some numbers are faster and well-organized to the point where they resemble a '40s big band on bad drugs; others could be an incompetent jazz combo vainly tuning up while someone sound checks the microphones (Robbins 1997 http://www.trouserpress.com/entry.php?a=tragic_mulatto, accessed October 25, 1997).

Similarly, on the Alternative Tentacles Web site, Tragic Mulatto is described as "[t]he dark and seedy underbelly of the average big city underbelly. A twilight zone for the already poorly adjusted" ("Description of Tragic Mulatto" www.alternativetentacles.com, accessed June 12, 1997).

Albums produced by Tragic Mulatto in the late 1980s as well as some other bands like The Beatnigs and Lard, all on Alternative Tentacles, were experimenting with new, nontraditional sounds and messages. By the mid to late 1990s many of the messages and musical styles on the three labels studied began to sound markedly different than anything we heard in the 1980s. Some of the bands producing records in the 1990s, however, continue to employ the traditional, relatively co-optable punk aesthetic.

We found more diversity among white males in the 1990s than in the 1980s. After the court case (noted earlier) that absorbed a year and a half of Jello Biafra's life, Biafra, the self-identified "information junkie," began going on lecture tours to college and university campuses. These lectures were and continue to be recorded and released on Alternative Tentacles. One of Biafra's spoken-word albums is sarcastically titled *High Priest of Harmful Matter*, derived from the charges against him ("distribution of harmful matter to minors"), and the record is mostly about his court case and censorship in general. *Beyond the Valley of the Gift Police*, a three-record spoken-word album released in 1994, was randomly sampled for this study. Most of the three-record set is a continuous talk on censorship given at Evergreen State College in Olympia, Washington, which has been cited throughout this study. Biafra continues to write and produce music. A few songs off his latest "Lard" album were randomly sampled. We have seen "Lard" categorized in music stores in San Francisco and Berkeley as "experimental." "Lard" has a very heavy, thick, deep heavy-metal sound coupled with Biafra's unique tremulous roar. The Lard album sampled, *Pure Chewing Satisfaction* (1997), comes with a large zine that has each song's lyrics surrounded by text and pictures highlighting dominant themes in the song, very similar to that described above by The Beatnigs. The following song, "Generation Execute," is typical of Biafra's anticonservative satire.

I went to Blockhead Video
To rent a tape of people makin' love
Couldn't find no love in here
'It's a family store, see here!'

Settled for 'Faces of Death'
But they'd rented it to some kid
I'm tired of the same old gore
Kick Butt Cable Network gives me more

All day
All night
Broadcast live

Gas
Fry

Injection
Die

Bring the pretzels, bring the kids
Have a party, have a beer
Phil Donahue got his wish
Executions on live TV

Here's your host, Kozy Kinkwicket!
What's your name?...You're 14?
And what are you being put to death for
today?
Is your family here?
What was your last meal?
Any last words for the fans?
Longer you cling to life—
More prizes for your friends

Gas
Fry
Yeh
Awright

What's it gonna be, old Sparky?
More points for the firing squad
Grand prize, step inside
The Hundred Thousand Dollar Gas Chamber

Answer the question:
How do we teach, 'Thou Shalt Not Kill?'
The gas is rising
There goes the bell

Five minutes...
Six minutes...
Ladies and gentlemen,
He's swallowing his tongue!

Vanna applauds

Lard, "Generation Execute," from album *Pure Chewing Satisfaction.*

The song protests the religious Right's influence over popular media, a topic covered at length on the spoken-word album, *Beyond the Valley of the Gift Police* (1994). Representative of the Dead Kennedys, Biafra employs satire to highlight contradictions within society and demonstrate their ludicrousness. In "Generation Execute," Biafra highlights contradictions within the religious Right, such as teaching not to kill while simultaneously endorsing killing through support of the death penalty, and teaching to love but banning love-making. Eugene Chadbourne & Evan Johns (1992), white males on Alternative Tentacles, also employ satire as a tactic to perpetuate protest messages, but they take a slightly different approach than Biafra.

Eugene Chadbourne & Evan Johns play a style of punk referred to on the Alternative Tentacles Web page as "[t]exan rock'n'roll originating from our nation's capitol. Old style garage rockabilly with guts and drive" (from bio on Chadbourne & Johns that appeared in http://www.alternativetentacles.com/, accessed October 25, 1997). With songs like "Achey Rakey Heart," "Redneck Jazz," and "Desert Storm Chewing Gum," Eugene Chadbourne & Evan Johns come across as funny country musicians protesting complex issues like war and consumerism.

The Leaving Trains also use satire, but it is often hard to determine what the messages are that they are attempting to promote. The Leaving Trains, led by Falling James, a white, male drag queen, have been around since the early 1980s recording on SST. On the album sampled for this study, *The Lump in My Forehead* (1992), the song "Women Are Evil" deals with issues not dealt with in the 1980s by white males on any of the three labels.

> women are evil
> lead ya down a road to death and destruction…
> make you feel like your two inches tall
>
> and then she goes in her cunt clothes all dressed to kill…
> I wanna fuck her
> but you won't let me…
>
> when you're a little boy…
> your mom says you're gonna grow up some day, you're gonna be a man
> and you say no mom I don't ever want to grow up…
> I wanna marry my best friend…
> but you grow up one day, and you get yourself a job
> and if you don't marry a woman,
> then you are a woman anyways…

> Excerpt from The Leaving Trains, "Women Are Evil," *The Lump in My Forehead,* SST 1992.

In our view, in "Women Are Evil," Falling James uses sexist content to denounce a sexist system. James shows how prescribed gender roles in the United States serve to create friction between men and women materializing in his life as hostility and mistrust toward women. This song could also possibly be an explanation for James's decision to dress in drag indicated by the line, "if you don't marry a woman, you're a woman anyways." We also recognize that by using sexist content, James reaffirms and perpetuates sexist messages even if attempting to protest socially prescribed gender roles.

Nonwhite males sang less about antiracism and love, were less sexist, and were coded more often as absent in the 1990s than in the 1980s (see Table 7.2, p. 91; another example of one of the authors' own white, male bias). In assembling the population parameters of the three labels and coding the 291 randomly sampled songs, we noticed that the collective group, "nonwhite males," consisted only of African Americans in the 1980s, but by the 1990s Japanese Americans, Mexicans, Mexican Americans, and other Latinos had entered the punk scene. Union 13 from East Los Angeles, for example, wove their life experiences as Latinos into a fairly traditional punk style. They were the brunt of criticism.

Note the following biography on Union 13 that appears on the Epitaph Web site.

> The arrogance of many club bookers, record labels and the media in the past has led the public to believe that Latino bands just aren't up to par with the American bands…'no one will be interested,' seemed to be the prevailing opinion. Well, they were certainly wrong; with the recent increase in record sales and sold-out shows by a variety of Latino bands, suddenly the music industry is up in arms about the 'rock en español' craze, and the Latino rock community is finally getting some of the respect and attention they deserve…They [Union 13] grew up in the Boyle Heights area of East Los Angeles, California, some of them in the toughest housing projects in the city (from the band's bio in http://www.epitaph.com/, accessed October 25, 1997).

The reference to American bands above suggests that the Latino in punk signifies something deviant, something other than real American punk. In trying to legitimate the band to skeptics, the author of the preceding biography of Union 13 plays into the hand of promoting the myth that poor kids and ethnic outsiders can make it big because the American dream happened to Union 13. In noting where in L.A. Union 13 grew up seems to do nothing more than give legitimacy to the false idea of meritocracy, the idea that hard work and determination will result in success. True, this highly political Latino band now has the chance to share their voices with a wider audience, but let us not forget that Epitaph is a corporation, and their discourse is constructed to sell music. After all, the author does make a point to mention that bands like Union 13 are becoming more popular and selling lots of records (for Epitaph). When Epitaph criticizes other record labels for not signing Latino bands, they do so by highlighting Latino bands marketability. This is the schizophrenic part of punk we found in looking at punk music as counterculture and protest, while at the same time enmeshed in making money. We argue that despite falling to all the temptations associated with the money part of the music industry, a lot of good, creative, and political energy continues to evolve in punk.

For example, Union 13's *East Los Presents*...front and back covers, the insert, and record itself are covered with writing styles, pictures, and other symbols that clearly mark the musicians as occupants of a Latino youth counterculture. On one side of the insert a group photo of the band is portrayed with one of the band members standing in front of the other members holding his fists in front of him with the band's name written across his knuckles in a geometric style derived from Latino youth countercultures. The lyrics tend to be written in either first person or a collective "we," implying a punk, Latino, male identity, assuming that "we" refers to others who share a similar identity. The song, "Final Approach" illustrates Union 13's usage of the collective "we."

> We're standing in back of the line and our time is running out. There's nothing we can do cuz we're living our lives with illusions and false hopes. We're the target of society...We don't believe this country stands for freedom. The only thing we see is a cell for you and me...Excerpt from Union 13, "Final Approach," *East Los Presents,* Epitaph Records 1997.

Here Edward, Union 13's singer in "Final Approach," protests and denounces an unjust and unequal world. The focus is on his social position as a poor Latino male youth, and as the target of deception and social injustice in a racist society. The song also could potentially speak to anyone who is aware of his/her own oppression. We are aware that there were other nonwhite males in the 1990s whose music offered similar perspectives, but do not appear in this study given our sampling selection.

Wesley Willis, an African American from Chicago, for example, who began hearing voices in 1989, started writing songs in 1992. Willis spent most of his adult life selling his drawings on the streets of Chicago. Willis, despite suffering from chronic schizophrenia, which was diagnosed in 1995, wrote over 400 songs. In 1995 Alternative Tentacles released *Wesley Willis Greatest Hits.* Willis plays with the heavy metal/punk rock band called the Wesley Willis Fiasco. All but two of the songs on his *Greatest Hits* record, consist only of his vocals and what sounds like a synthesizer/drum machine. In our content analysis, most of the songs coded on this record were coded as absent. Mentally ill people, because of the stigma of mental illness, tend to be a marginalized group in U.S. society and are rarely heard. The following song, "Chronic Schizophrenia," was coded as absent, but we nonetheless consider it an important song.

> My mind plays tricks on me every time I say something
> It brings evil voices out of my head and talks to me vulgar
> Then suddenly I started raving
> Chronic Schizophrenia
> Chronic Schizophrenia
> Chronic Schizophrenia
> Chronic Schizophrenia…
>
> But when I have bad luck, I always hear evil voices talking to me vulgar
> Everywhere I go riding on the CTA bus all I hear is vulgarity I hear no music at all
> Chronic Schizophrenia
> Chronic Schizophrenia
> Chronic Schizophrenia
> Chronic Schizophrenia…
>
> Riding the streets with no music sucks
> Everywhere I go I cruise the streets being called an asshole plus I'm being ridiculed being called a bum and stupid
> Chronic Schizophrenia
> Chronic Schizophrenia
> Chronic Schizophrenia
> Chronic Schizophrenia…
>
> Wesley Willis Fiasco, "Chronic Schizophrenia," from album *Wesley Willis Greatest Hits.*
>

In this song, Willis gives voice to a perspective in U.S. society rarely heard. His voice humanizes those identified as mentally ill.

Our own experiences in dealing with the medical profession and other service providers for the mentally ill reflects society's attitude toward the mentally ill as burdens to society, as throwaways. They are not considered productive or useful citizens in an economic and political system where people are not individuals but cogs in a wheel. What matters is that they perform with efficiency and without problems or glitches to the overall workings of society. The lyrics in the song "Chronic Schizophrenia" personalize mentally ill people and sends the message that they are real people with real problems who hurt and feel pain and whose illness speaks of society's imperfections. Similarly, African American, former Black Panther, current Pennsylvania Death Row inmate (for a crime he did not commit), father, grandfather, husband, and lifetime revolutionary journalist, Mumia Abu-Jamal, and others like him stand as voices crying in the wilderness. His music released on Alternative Tentacles, like Willis's, unmasks the everyday lived realities of racism, society's throwaways, and the political and economic contradictions that ignore them.

In 1997 Alternative Tentacles released *Mumia Abu-Jamal: Spoken Word with Music by Man Is the Bastard.* The first 12 tracks are commentaries by Mumia Abu-Jamal and statements by Assata Shakur, Bob Dole, Allen Ginsburg, and Jello Biafra. The last four tracks are songs by the punk rock band Man Is the Bastard that have a dark, heavy sound, often with growling incoherent vocals. On the "Man Is the Bastard" part of the insert after the lyrics to the songs, the band thanked Mumia Abu-Jamal for letting them work with him and coming together for a common cause. In the Mumia Abu-Jamal part of the insert, on 16 out of 20 pages, Noelle Hanrahan, director of The Prison Radio Project/ Quixote Center, and Jane Henderson, director of the Equal Justice USA/ Quixote Center, explains who Mumia Abu-Jamal is and why he is on Death Row; and situates his story in an historical socioeconomic/political context. The following overview of Mumia's story is a summary from track transcripts that included an argument by Jane Henderson for why Mumia Abu-Jamal should be granted a retrial.

Mumia Abu-Jamal was Minister of Information for the Philadelphia chapter of the Black Panther Party (BPP) when he was 15 years old. After the BPP was successfully destroyed (many believe by the FBI with local law enforcement agencies), Mumia Abu-Jamal continued his journalism through broadcasting and became well known and respected for his world-class work, becoming one of the top names in local Pennsylvania radio. Mumia, however, lost many jobs because of his uncompromising use of revolutionary journalism obtained from the BPP_in short, for being "too black." Many activists continue to advocate for the release of Mumia or a commutation of the death sentence. The content of the album consists mostly of Mumia providing excellent critical critiques of the criminal justice system in the United States and its interconnectedness with colonialism, capitalism, and its role in maintaining the status quo_that status quo being white supremacy and the oppression of peoples of color. The songs by Man Is the Bastard are calls to action that complement Mumia Abu-Jamal's commentaries. A collection of Mumia's commentaries were supposed to be aired on National Public Radio's (NPR) *All Things Considered*, but were cancelled after the Fraternal Order of Police threatened NPR's funding. Those commentaries are now available on Alternative Tentacles on an album called *All Things Censored* (2000), and are also included with Mumia's most recent book, his third book written from the most punitive section of society, death row, also called *All Things Censored* (2000).

These two albums, as well as the three books he has written, all of which he has been punished for writing, are therefore an important tool for liberating Mumia Abu-Jamal's voice, hopefully his body, from brutal solitary confinement. Mumia's cause is part of Alternative Tentacles' effort to fight censorship and expose the United States for what it is, an unjust white supremacist system that serves to dehumanize people and that its ultimate purpose is to exploit their labor power. It is not what it claims itself to be—a godly state that imparts good will and freedom to the world.

The *Mumia Abu-Jamal/Man Is the Bastard* split is not the only recent project of significance Jello Biafra and Alternative Tentacles have embarked on. In 1997 Alternative Tentacles released *Who Bombed Judi Bari?: Judi Bari Spoken Word...with Music too!* Judi Bari died March 2, 1997 of breast cancer. Bari spent her adult life as a social activist defending abortion clinics, advocating for working people, and fighting to save old growth forests to name a few of the social issues she fought for. Bari's last efforts were with Earth First!, a radical environmental group. Bari helped many environmentalists see how environmental issues and worker issues are inseparable. She argued that multinational corporations are simultaneously exploiting and destroying the world and its inhabitants. Most of the tracks on the record are various talks Bari gave at demonstrations, on the radio, from the hospital she was in after being car bombed, and from various universities and colleges. There are four twangy folk songs on the album sung by Judi and others. The only thing punk about the record is the label it's on. But

Judi Bari's sense of humor and radicalism is not unlike that of many punk artists on Alternative Tentacles.

Like Mumia Abu-Jamal's album, Bari's record is an important tool that could possibly serve to reach people who would not otherwise hear about Earth First! Since we did the content analysis for this book two years ago, Alternative Tentacles has released a slew of lecture CDs by leading political analysts, activists, and university professors such as Noam Chomsky, Howard Zinn, and Angela Davis. These records will not only further radicalize punk rockers and the spaces they create, but will hopefully also draw support from individuals who would not normally support Alternative Tentacles and other independent labels. Further, these lecture records are evidence of a growing connection between traditional and organic intellectuals.

Alternative Tentacles has also been increasingly opening its cultural space to women who express alternative sexual identities such as Tribe 8. The song "Butch in the Streets" from Tribe 8's first Alternative Tentacles release, *Fist City* (1995), illustrates the messages these San Francisco–based, self-proclaimed "hardcore punker dykes" perpetuate.

struttin' on an i-beam in her steel toes and tool belt
tellin' all the boys what to do
takes off her hardhat
runs her hand through her crewcut
but don't let all those muscles fool you
she's a walkin' paradox in her jeans and her docs
sportin' big ugly tattoos
she goes home throws her legs in the air
hopin' no one heard the news

she's butch in the streets femme in the sheets
she's just a girl when she gets home
she wants to get plowed just like anyone else
don't let her fool you she's femme to the bone
butch in the streets femme in the sheets
butch in the streets femme in the sheets
butch in the streets femme in the sheets
walking' down the street in her leather at night
you like the way she mounts that harley-davidson bike
jump on the back
she gives it a rev
don't think she's gonna top you cuz she's belly up in bed
she's butch in the streets

femme in the sheets
she's just a girl when she gets home
she wants to get plowed like anyone else
don't let her fool you she's femme to the bone
butch in the streets femme in the sheets

Tribe 8, "Butch in the Streets," from album *Fist City*.

We coded Tribe 8's "Butch in the Streets" as homosexual, social protest, and sexist.

Lynn Breedlove, Tribe 8's singer, throughout the entire song protests dominant conceptions of sexuality by expressing an affirmation of homosexuality in an increasingly conservative social context marked by overt acts of homophobia such as universities refusing to grant same-sex partner benefits, the brutal murder of Mathew Shepard, and so forth. Breedlove also protests dominant conceptions of maleness and femaleness by portraying women in positions of power over men and doing work traditionally thought of as men's work. However, in so doing Breedlove simply replaces the male body traditionally in the oppressor role with a female body, failing to announce a new, more just, less exploitative reality. This discourse might feel empowering, but it still perpetuates the idea of sex-based inequality and was therefore coded as sexist in our analysis. The "femme/butch" dichotomy Breedlove perpetuates suggests a relationship of domination and subordination, which in our view portrays the women in the song as sexist by sexually dominating other women.

By contrast, some argue that punk simply creates a space that challenges society's tendency to label and force people to live within prescribed societal boundaries. In a roundtable discussion with three Asian women punkers, Margarita Alcantara, Leslie Mah, and Selena Whang, which was published in an article titled "Yellowdykecore: Queer, Punk 'n' Asian," Alcantara, Mah, and Whang argue that punk rock is "more about androgyny" (1997, 217), though admittedly they talked about being punk as a way to negotiate being queer in a society that rejects them as lesbians and as Asians. Leslie Mah (lead guitarist of Tribe 8) noted: "if I dyed my hair blue and shaved the side of my head, then, you know, boys wouldn't pay any attention to me in that kind of sexual way, and I wouldn't have to worry about dating boys or having to play that heterosexual game. So, in a way, it was sort of a cover-up for being queer, too" (Alcantara, et al. 1997, 217).

Adding to her comments above, Mah also noted:

> I think it's really good to come up with some sort of definition like, 'This is what it is to be a lesbian, this is what it is to be Chinese,' so you can go find other people with those characteristics, and you can start this community, and you can be strong. You know who you are, you have the definition. But then several years down the line a lot of people will say, 'Fuck these definitions, they're so rigid, I'm not going to label myself a lesbian because of the fucking definitions.' People see you just this one way. So, defining who you are is a really powerful thing, but then, eventually you have to smash all those definitions, continue to rebuild it, and start all over again (p. 223).

We suggest throughout this book that it is this smashing of definitions that characterizes what punk and punk rock is all about. Thus, punk as an identity and as a political community underscores the point that "as a dynamic process, the social construction of community offers the possibility for redefinition of boundaries, for broadened constituencies, and for seemingly unlikely alliances" (Naples 1998, 337). As Margarita Alcantara, Leslie Mah, and Selena Whang show, new forms of punk are evolving, but still rooted in the hope of revolutionizing society.

Chapter 9

Conclusion: The Inevitable Revolution

Unlike the mainstream music business, which frequently experiences stylistic changes in an effort to sell more records and increase capital (Frith 1982), the punk rock labels in this study experienced changes in an effort to perhaps prevent co-optation and maintain opportunities for alternative perspectives and identities. Much of the current punk rock we looked at for this study seems to still be out of corporate reach, both stylistically and politically. As a result, what underground, nonmainstream punk rock was during the 1980s tends not to be what it is today, and what underground, nonmainstream punk rock is today will probably not be what it will be tomorrow. While it is true that change happens, we cannot overemphasize the continuity between mainstream and alternative. They are not dichotomous, but are meshed together in subtle ways. As a result of being socialized in U.S. society, we internalize the ideas, values, and beliefs of the ruling class (i.e., race and belief in capitalism), promoted through cultural institutions such as the mass media. Thus, we have to constantly struggle against it by engaging in the lifelong process of naming, reflecting, and acting. But we recognize that when we work to create counterhegemonic spaces and cultures, elements of the hegemonic structure inevitably also reemerges. Few of us escape the fact that we live in a white society, a society that teaches that we are superior to other humans. That is precisely why many radicals also become preoccupied with fighting and judging each other. As advocates of social change and social justice it is our job to courageously show real respect to those in our struggles. We must also not forget that there are people who will hurt us if given the chance, but we cannot lose hope, for humans have the ability to be conscious of their own consciousness (Freire 1970b). We are taught to view the world in false dichotomies, black/white, capitalism/socialism, man/woman, liberal/conservative, and so forth, which serves to divide people. By focusing on the extremities, the more mainstream perspectives and the more alternative perspectives begin to resemble dichotomies. To be human is to create (Freire 1970b).

As such, punk has branched and merged taking on new meanings as it forges new styles and opens up to a wider variety of people and meshes with mainstream concepts in new ways. For example, the more than ten lecture/spoken-word releases on Alternative Tentacles, many of which are double and triple albums, from prominent academics, activists, and revolutionaries, represents a strong alliance with radical traditional intellectuals. The impact of punk will continue for years to come. It is a product of the changing face of alternative cultural spaces. It is becoming harder and harder to classify, generalize about, and label punk now than it was in the 1980s.

However, as we read and listened to both earlier and current punk, patterns did emerge as previously discussed (see Tables 7.2, p. 91; and 7.5, p. 94). What is clear is that punk rock and the cultural spaces it has created are now taking on new meanings for more people than they ever have before. What are the implications of the increased heterogeneity of punk? Is punk becoming increasingly fragmented and disparate? Or is the diversity a reflection of the punk rock community's general concern for democracy, social justice, and building solidarity in an increasingly capitalist, hostile, violent, racist, and sexist world? Due to the relative absence of accommodating content in the 1990s, we are advocating for an argument for the latter. As Arlene Stein (1997) commented on the increasing heterogeneity of the lesbian community in the United Sataes: "today's more 'decentered' movement may present new democratic potential" (pp. 389–390). It is therefore up to us, the scholars, the artists, the musicians, the journalists, to acknowledge difference and to reveal inconsistencies and injustices. Together we have to challenge others to challenge and to name, reflect, and act on the ideas, values, and beliefs we have and continue to internalize as products of a dominantly white, heterosexist, capitalist society.

As a white, middle-class man, I, Curry Malott, cannot stress enough my own positionality as a white, middle-class man. And as a Latina woman, I, Milagros Peña, while sharing much with Curry, see and feel the punk genre much more directly in its racial and sexist contradictions. Nonetheless, together we recognize how our positionalities in our heterosexual identities impact how we see ourselves in the world in relation to others and their ever-changing perspectives such as, for example, "butch in the streets." Our critiques, in both their strengths and limitations herein are therefore no different than any other critiques in that our particular positionalities, worldviews, and incomplete selves inform them. With that in mind, there is no way we could or would desire to limit reality of our critiques and interpretations to a single perspective. We are now two people of relative privilege with one who lived a life free of many existing oppressions (racism and sexism). Despite that limitation, we now consciously together with others, live to produce counterhegemonic spaces (while still recognizing the privileges we continue to benefit from). Confronting such privileges is a perspective important to discourse for other whites struggling with their own internalized oppressive baggage, which includes racism and sexism. It is also important for traditionally oppressed groups in the United States such as African Americans, Latinos/as, First Nations people, to be aware of the existence of and to dialogue with progressive whites who are wholeheartedly allies and not enemies (Tatum 1997). Our critiques should not be read as an attempt to speak for others or to rigidly define some parameters of reality based on our perspectives, but as a statement of how we see the world. With this reasoning, it was our intention throughout this book to foster dialogue and to open lines of communication, and not to self-righteously judge others, thus creating more mistrust and closing opportunities for communication. We are not apologizing for words we have written, we are simply saying let us work together in the name of justice if we are to build a better, more humane world.

Afterword

Remaking the Revolution

The power and promise of collective struggle exemplified by Quetzal, a nine-piece band with bragging rights as arguably Los Angeles's premier Latino/a musical group, is a feature that is not found much any more in the corporatized and businessified world of music. Quetzal's blend of Zapatista politics and what has been described as "*jarocho* hip" musical style is about as far away from punk rock as one could imagine. Closer to the punk sensibility perhaps are the *narcocorridos perrones* with their ranchero influence (their accordion-driven *norteno* style, or brass-based *banda* style), inspired by "El Gallo de Sinaloa," Chalino Sanchez, who was gunned down by police during a concert tour in Culiacan. For *Chalinitos* such as Jessie Morales, Lupillo Rivera, or Jenni Rivera, a celebration of the world of sex and drugs, shootouts with the law, betrayal and contraband, is close to the punk creed. What links all of this music together is a grand refusal of the American dream, whether this dream comes in the form of the North American Free Trade Agreement or the promise of a secure factory job with medical benefits and a row house in a blue-collar district. Surely the punkers of today can readily identify with Juan Rivera's lyrics: "*Hoy vamos amanecernos con el diablo entre las venas*" (translated as "today we are going to awaken with the devil in our veins").

Combining hard data with critical sociology and personal narratives, *Punk Rockers' Revolution* by Curry Malott and Milagros Peña speaks to the raw emotions, the rage, and the street-spawned and knife-edged cultural insights of the punk phenomenon. They raise the question of the extent to which punk is a potentially revolutionary, countercapitalist stance, and whether or not punkers may have an (albeit limited) claim to the Gramscian role of organic intellectual. This may seem an exaggerated claim to some readers familiar with the stereotype of punkers as white racist skinheads. Readily admitting and condemning the underlying racism and white supremacy that continues to provide ideological ballast to a significant amount of punk music and the punk lifestyle, the authors also explore some of the liberating possibilities latent in the politics of punk music, as well as the more emancipating tropes and conceits visible in its newly emerged revolutionary codicil. As to the possibility of the transmogrification of punk into a bona fide oppositional movement, the authors cite the example of some working-class punk bands in England establishing links with the Socialist Workers Party. But the book is not an attempt to test the coevality of punk as racist/antiracist or liberating/progressive. It is, rather, a scholarly attempt to provide a nuanced understanding of punk beyond its stereotypical depiction.

The authors remind us that it is important to remember that punk is not only the music of garbage collectors, factory workers, and those who work at McDonalds or Burger King, but is also the music of choice of middle-class skateboarders. Skaterpunk began when white male punkers—who often identified as suburban burnouts—co-opted the skateboarding phenomenon. It is increasingly the case that as a musical culture, punk cannot be considered as static or homogeneous, but now demonstrates different class, gender, ethnic, cultural, and political inflections. The authors note that while, early on, punk embraced decidedly white working-class concepts of masculinity and hardness, punk is increasingly becoming a hybrid, multicultural, and potentially revolutionary form of human expression. The authors maintain that punk rockers in the United States comprise a heterogeneous group with often disparate political orientations and worldviews that vary with the contextual specificity of regional geography and time periods.

When Greg Graffin of the group, Bad Religion, sang "modern man destroy yourself in shame, modern man pathetic example of earth's organic heritage, just a sample of carbon-based waste, just a fucking tragic epic of you and I," on their 1990's *Against the Grain* album, he was asserting the perennial punk theme of social protest. Malott and Peña's detailed analysis of 1980's and 1990's punk rock lyrics brings to light the importance of punk not only as a musical genre, but also as a form of social protest. In its analysis of the music of the punk counterculture, it provides both a statistical and descriptive optic to the punk phenomenon.

The keening of Marx's followers gathered at his gravesite, hoping to resurrect some revolutionary commitment from the social movements his analysis once engendered, are drowned out by the fierce shrieks of delight stabbing the cigar-spiked air in the hallways of corporate power. The CEOs who steer the fate of the transnational elite continue to celebrate the world-historical disappearance of the old bearded devil. Marx would no doubt turn in his grave to think that punk would become part of his legacy of protest (*de omnibus dubitandum, doubt everything* [his favorite motto]. Perhaps his horror would be mollified somewhat by the recognition that there isn't much current opposition to capital's law of value or dissention from the path of neoliberalism, at least in the developed nations of the West who have embraced the rule of capital as the "end of history." But isn't what the punks are reacting against precisely what Marx termed "alienated labor"—the estranged labor that separates individuals from what Marx called their "species life." Under capitalism we are denied our capacity to produce in response to need but also in response to freedom from need. Aren't punks, at some level, reacting to their imprisonment within the global factory, within the social universe of capital, where life is lived in subordination to the commodity circuit, intensified by the global mobility of finance capital and the reconstitution of the industrial working class in global *maquiladoras*. Aren't punks reacting to the colonization of their subjectivities by the cultural logic of late capitalism, to the subsumption of their social roles within the commodity logic of dead labor? Doesn't punk still recruit from Marx's reserve army of labor? Will punks be prominent as the future gravediggers of capital? In this sense, couldn't punk be considered as a form of unmaterialized revolutionary potential?

The authors are especially good at explaining how some of the major turning points in punk were heavily influenced by corresponding periods of sociopolitical depression. Fat Mike, of NOFX and *Fat Wreckords*, seems to agree, stating recently that the only positive thing that will come of the current Bush administration will be all of the great punk music.

The comments of Fat Mike are chillingly apposite given the living infrastructure of alienated labor that is helping to promote the current transition of the United States into a garrison state. We have the USA Patriot Act, we have the military tribunals, we have the Office of Homeland Security, we have the necessary scapegoats, we have the Office of Strategic Influence working hand-in-hand with the U.S. Army's Psychological Operations Command (PSYOPS) operating domestically. Actually, operating domestically is against the law, but we know that during the Reagan administration that PSYOPS staffed the Office of Public Diplomacy and planted stories in the media supporting the Contras, a move made possible by Otto Reich, now the assistant secretary of state for Western Hemisphere Affairs. We know that a few years ago members of PSYOPS were discovered working as interns in the news division of CNN's Atlanta headquarters. We have the strongest military in the world. We have the military hawks in control of the Pentagon. We have recently pummeled two evil nations into prehistory, and identified new evil and quasi-evil empires. We have turned Central Asia into a zone of military containment, and shown that we can kill mercilessly and control the media reporting in the theater of operations, as major newspapers regularly buried stories of U.S. air strikes and killings of innocent civilians. And we have a leader who is little more than a glorified servant of the military industrial complex—one who is able to admit this publicly and arouse little opposition. In fact, such an admission wins him the glowing admiration of the American people. The Bush administration's scheduled release of documents under the Presidential Records Act of 1978, which includes Ronald Reagan's papers, have successfully been placed on lockdown. Thus far Cheney's much publicized legal stonewalling has prevented full disclosure of the extent of Enron-National Energy Policy Development Group contacts. Government secrecy and the withholding of information available to the public by law has become a guiding axiom of government practice. If this isn't a time ripe for the diatribes of punk outrage, we are hard-pressed to identify what is.

One of the negative features of punk identified by the authors is that punks are too preoccupied with issues of authenticity. Here, punk becomes reduced to an identity-based movement that frequently falls into the trap of integralism, or the desire for a totalizing identity, for a master formula that provides all the necessary characteristics of the punk reality. Too often such integralism has manifested itself in the tropes of white supremacy, homophobia, and violence against women. These aspects of punk are not to be overlooked or pushed aside in any attempt to identify the potential of punk as a force contesting dominant social relations of exploitation.

Punk Rockers' Revolution explores the manner in which and the extent to which punk constitutes a revolutionary countercapitalist stance, and how it continues to combat capitalist domination with its attendant manifestations of racism and sexism. The authors admit that while the evolution of punk has not, as yet, resulted in anything close to what could be considered a social movement, it nevertheless reflects, in its best incarnations, a concerted countercultural struggle for social justice and humanization. We are provided with a detailed look at the singular contribution to the development of punk made by Jello Biafra, owner of the Alternative Tentacles punk record label, and a former Dead Kennedy. For instance, Biafra often employs satire to protest the religious Right in the popular media and to highlight the contradictions within society, demonstrating its expanding dimensions of ludicrousness. He also publishes lectures by Noam Chomsky, Howard Zinn, and Angela Davis. The authors also undertake a content analysis of punk lyrics in order to illuminate the intricate interconnections of norms and values of six subgroups of punks and those of the dominant society, and to highlight general message trends over time. They offer a persuasive argument that punk music and culture has evolved from the homogeneous, loud, uniform, repetitive, white male protest against the dominant society. They describe punk as "fluid and historically contingent, best characterized as a cultural space rather than as a musical style. It is no longer just one style, but a place, one of the only places where groups and individuals with varying styles can express ideas and tell stories that would not be heard otherwise" (p. 154). One of the important lessons that we learn is that punk's roots are clearly white, male, and heterosexual. But we also learn that there is not only an emerging queer punk scene, that African Americans entered the punk scene by the 1980s, followed a decade later by Japanese Americans, Mexican Americans, and other Latino/a groups. All these groups are reacting to their specific location—both culturally and in terms of the capitalist social relations—within a racist, sexist, and exploitative social system. For instance, aren't the new Chicano punkers reacting to their positioning as diasporic reservoirs of labor power—human residue from recent transnational configurations of gangster capitalism, the casualties of El Norte's superexploitation of the toilers of El Sud?

Critical pedagogy does not dwell on how much we are alienated from our past as much as how much we are alienated from our own potential future as agents with the creative capacity to make our actions the object of our will. In doing so, we engage in the revolutionary activity of remaking the social order. Even though punkers have upped the stakes with mohawk haircuts and leather, in their attempt to resist conservatives from co-opting the genre, this is not an easy task at a time when the transnational capitalist elite continues to gain ground. Multinational record companies proceed unimpeded in their attempts to buy out small punk labels. It is only the most radical punk bands that tend not to be absorbed by the mainstream who achieve corporate success—but then they forfeit their claim to punkness (the authors point out that it is conceptually impossible to be a punk millionaire).

With the publication of *Punk Rockers' Revolution*, punks again have something to scream about. This book fits well with our own understanding, and appreciation, of punk. It will educate the nonpunk about punk culture, both the positive and negative aspects, and it will cause punks to look at or study punk in a new light. Like a good punk album, this book hopes to open your eyes, piss you off, and make you think.

Peter McLaren and Jonathan McLaren
Los Angeles, California, and College Station, Maryland

Appendix

The following instructions were employed to guide coding. Coding instructions were borrowed primarily from a dissertation entitled "The Message in the Music: A Content Analysis of Contemporary Christian and Southern Gospel Song Lyrics" (1987) by Gary Richard Drum.

Coding Instructions

- This study is based on the evaluation "of the *entire* lyric, so read the entire lyric at least twice before proceeding, then make your evaluation on the entire lyric *as a whole*" (Drum 1987, 104).
- Certain songs may contain contradictory categories, such as songs that contain both sexist and antisexist messages. If you code a similar song, code it as both sexist and antisexist.
- You may also come across a song that derides the federal government on the basis of supporting racial/ethnic minorities. Such a song would be coded as containing the following two messages: social protest and racism. Or, you may come across a song that derides the federal government on the basis of subjugating racial/ethnic minorities. Such a song would be coded as both social protest and antiracism.
- When in doubt of the presence of a particular category circle, "absent." For example, if you are not sure if the song has sexist content, circle "absent."
- "Since themes may only occur once in a song, you should continually refer to the lyric as you go along" (Drum 1987, 104).
- "Under each theme listed are one or more examples of phrases that have been found to be used to express these themes. This is *not* an [exhaustive] list" (Drum 1987, 104).
- "Work continuously, going from lyric to lyric, being sure to indicate [song number, gender of message presenter, race or ethnicity of message presenter if identifiable, and year song was published]. There is no set time limit, but work at an even pace" (Drum 1987, 104).

- Code record labels in the following way: Alternative Tentacles (1), SST (2), Epitaph (3).

Code Form

Song #___ List #___
Date song published 1980s (1)__ 1990s (2)__
Sex of singer: female (1)__ male (0)__
Race/Ethnicity of singer (check one)
White (0)___
Nonwhite (1)___

Record label #___
1.) Social protest content in song (circle one)
absent (0) present (1)

2.) Antiracist content in song (circle one)
absent (0) present (1)

3.) Antisexist content in song (circle one)
absent (0) present (1)

4.) Anti-love/romance content in song (circle one)
absent (0) present (1)

5.) Homosexual content in song (circle one)
absent (0) present (1)

6.) Antisocial protest content in song (circle one)
absent (0) present (1)

7.) Racist content in song (circle one)
absent (0) present (1)

8.) Sexist content in song (circle one)
absent (0) present (1)

9.) Love/romantic content in song (circle one)
absent (0) present (1)

10.) Homophobic content in song (circle one)
absent (0) present (1)

11.) "Absent" content in song (circle one)
absent (0) present (1)

Notes

Chapter 2

1 Fanzines are "...publications devoted exclusively to topics of interest to punks, and generally related to the punk music scene..." (Henry, 1989, 93). In addition, fanzines, by definition, are created by punks usually at little to no cost, and they tend to rely heavily on letters from fans and musicians for personal narratives and the creation of a discourse, which serves to build community.

Chapter 3

1 "His-story" was used in the chapter title for emphasis because the vantage point of privileged white males in presenting the history of popular music was assumed and unquestioned by the majority of scholars we consulted for this discussion.

2 Fanzine: small magazines usually an amalgam of text and pictures, drawings, etc., photocopied on paper created by punks for punks with the intention of creating an avenue for discourse outside the boundaries of dominant discourse for individuals who would otherwise be unheard.

Chapter 4

1 Traditionally, punk music is created by punks for punks at little cost and often requiring little skill.

Chapter 5

1 "The Fonz" was a character on *Happy Days* that was portrayed as an occupant of a biker counterculture, but his values and beliefs were not unlike those characters portrayed as occupants of mainstream culture.

Chapter 6

1 Categories are operationalized as mutually exclusive and will therefore be substantiated simultaneously. For example, by substantiating the use of sexism, we will simultaneously be substantiating the use of antisexism.

References

Abu-Jamal, Mumia. 1995. *Live from Death Row*. New York: Avon Books.

___ 1996. *Death Blossoms: Reflections from a Prisoner of Conscience*. Farmington, PA: Plough Publishing House.

___ 2000. *All Things Censored*. New York: Seven Stories.

Abu-Jamal, Mumia, and Man Is the Bastard. 1997. *Mumia Abu-Jamal: Spoken Word with Music by Man Is the Bastard*. San Francisco: Alternative Tentacles, Virus 206.

Adorno, Theodor W. 1989. "On the Fetish Character in Music and the Regression of Listening." In *The Essential Frankfurt School Reader*, edited by Arato, Andrew and Eike Gebhardt, 270–299. New York: Continuum.

Albelda, Randy, Elaine McCrate, Edwin Melendez, June Lapidus, and The Center for Popular Economics. 1988. *Mink Coats Don't Trickle Down: The Economic Attack on Women and People of Color*. Boston, MA: South End Press.

Alcantara, Margarita, Leslie Mah, and Selena Whang. 1997. "Yellowdykecore: Queer, Punk 'n' Asian: A Roundtable Discussion." In *Dragon Ladies: Asian American Feminists Breathe Fire*, edited by Sonia Shah, 216–232. Boston, MA: South End Press.

"Description of 'Tragic Mulatto.'" 1997. *Alternative Tentacles Web Site*. www.alternativetentacles.com, accessed June 12, 1997.

Arato, Andrew and Eike Gebhardt (Editors). 1989. *The Essential Frankfurt School Reader*. New York: Continuum.

Armaline, William D., Kathleen S. Farber, and Shan Nelson-Rowe. "Reading Class: Marxist Theories of Education." 1994. In *From the Left Bank to the Mainstream: Historical Debates and Contemporary Research in Marxist Sociology*, edited by Patrick McGuire and Donald McQuarie, 178–206. New York: General Hall Publishing Company.

Aronowitz, Stanley, and Henry Giroux. 1985. *Education under Siege*. South Hadley, MA: Bergin and Garvey.

___ 1993. *Education Still under Siege*. South Hadley, MA: Bergin and Garvey.

Austin, Joe, Michael Willard. 1998. *Generations of Youth: Youth Cultures and History in Twentieth-Century America*. New York: New York University Press.

Babbie, Earl. 1995. *The Practice of Social Research*. Belmont, CA: Wadsworth Publishing Company.

Bari, Judi. 1997. *Who Bombed Judi Bari?: Judi Bari Spoken Word...with Music Too!* San Francisco: Alternative Tentacles, Virus 205.

Baudrillard, Jean. 1995. *The Mirror of Production*, St. Louis, MO: Telos Press.

Bennett, Stith H., Jeff Ferrell. 1987. "Music Videos and Epistemic Socialization." *Youth and Society* 18, 4: 344–362.

Berry, Millard, Ralph Franklin, Alan Franklin, Cathy Kauflin, Marilyn Werbe, Richard Wieske, and Peter Werbe. 1974. *Wildcat: dodge truck june 1974*. Detroit, MI: Black & Red.

Biafra, Jello. 1994. *Beyond the Valley of the Gift Police: Spoken Word Album #4*. San Francisco: Alternative Tentacles Records, Virus 150.

___ 1997. "Sucking in the '70s—Again." Translated by John Pecorelli. *Alternative Press Magazine* 110 (September): 96.

Biafra, Jello, and Mojo Nixon with the Toadliquors. 1994. *Prairie Home Invasion*. San Francisco: Alternative Tentacles Records, Virus 137.

Bin Wahad, Dhoruba, Assata Shakur, and Mumia Abu-Jamal. 1993. *Still Black, Still Strong: Survivors of the War Against Black Revolutionaries*. New York: Automedia.

Black Panther Party. "Liberation Schools." In *The Black Panthers Speak*, edited by Philip S. Foner. New York: Da Capo Press, [1969] 1995.

Callinicos, Alex. 1993. *Race and Class*. London: Bookmarks.

Carey, James T. 1969a. "The Ideology of Autonomy in Popular Lyrics: A Content Analysis." *Psychiatry: Journal for the Study of International Processes*, 32, no. 2: 150–164.

___ 1969b. "Changing Courtship Patterns in Popular Song." *The American Journal of Sociology* 74, no. 4: 720–731.

Castells, Manuel. 1998. *End of Millennium*. Oxford: Blackwell.

Chadbourne, Eugene, and Evan Johns. 1992. "Terror Has Some Strange Kinfolk." San Francisco: Alternative Tentacles, Virus 119.

___ Alternative Tentacles Bio. 1997. http://www.alternativetentacles.com/, accessed October 25.

Chávez Chávez, Rudolfo (Editor). 1998. *Speaking the Unpleasant*. New York: State University of New York Press.

Chomsky, Noam, and Edward Herman. 1988. *Manufacturing Consent: The Political Economy of the Mass Media*. New York: Pantheon Books.

Churchill, Ward, and Jim Vander Wall. 1990a. *Agents of Repression: The FBI's Secret Wars against the Black Panther Party and the American Indian Movement*. Boston: South End Press.

___ 1990b. *The COINTELPRO Papers: Documents from the FBI's Secret Wars against Dissent in the United States*. Boston: South End Press.

Cohen, Jean L., and Andrew Arato. 1992. *Civil Society and Political Theory*. Cambridge, MA: MIT Press.

Cohen, Philip. [1972] 1980. "Subcultural Conflict and Working-Class Community." In *Culture, Media, Language: Working Papers in Cultural Studies 1972–79*, edited by Stuart Hall, Dorothy Hobson, Andrew Lowe, and Paul Willis. Birmingham: The Centre for Contemporary Cultural Studies, University of Birmingham, 78–87.

Cole, Richard R. 1971. "Top Songs in the Sixties: A Content Analysis of Popular Lyrics." *American Behavioral Scientist* 14, no. 3: 389–400.

Corrigan, Philip. 1989. "Playing...Contra/dictions, Empowerment and Embodiment: Punk, Pedagogy, and Popular Cultural Forms (On Ethnography and Education)." In *Popular Culture: Schooling and Everyday Life,* edited by Henry Giroux and Roger Simon. New York: Bergin & Garvey, 67–90.

Dancis, Bruce. 1978. "Safety Pins and Class Struggle: Punk Rock and the Left." *Socialist Review* 8, no. 39: 58–83.

Davies, Jude. 1994. "The Future of 'No Future': Punk Rock and Postmodern Theory." *Journal of Popular Culture* 29: 4 (Spring): 3–25.

Dead Kennedys. 1980. *California Über Alles*. San Francisco: Alternative Tentacles, Virus 0.

___ 1980. *Fresh Fruit for Rotting Vegetables.* San Francisco: Alternative Tentacles, Virus 1.

___ 1985. *Frankenchrist.* San Francisco: Alternative Tentacles, Virus 45.

DeMott, Benj. 1988. "The Future Is Unwritten: Working-Class Youth Cultures in England and America." *Critical Texts* 5 no. 1: 42–56.

Denisoff, Serge R. 1971. *Great Day Coming: Folk Music and the American Left.* Baltimore, MD: Penguin Books.

Descendents. 1987. *All.* Lawndale, CA: SST, 112.

___ 1987. *I Don't Want to Grow Up.* Lawndale, CA: SST, 143.

Dixon, Richard D., Fred R. Ingram, Richard M. Levinson, and Catherine L. Putnam. 1979. "The Cultural Diffusion of Punk Rock in the United States." *Popular Music and Society*, 6: 3: 210–218.

Doggin. 1996. "A Conversation with Duane and some of Sacto's finest," *Heckler Magazine*, www.heckler.com/4.2tw/duane.html, accessed October 25, 1997.

Domhoff, G. William. 2003. *Changing The Powers That Be: How The Left Can Stop Losing and Win.* New York: Rowman & Littlefield Publishers, Inc.

Dreeben, Robert. 1968. *On What Is Learned in School.* Reading, MA: Addison-Wesley.

Drum, Gary Richard. 1987. "The Message in the Music: A Content Analysis of Contemporary Christian and Southern Gospel Song Lyrics." Ph.D. diss., University of Tennessee.

Edwards, Richard. 1979. *Contested Terrain: The Transformation of the Workplace in the Twentieth Century.* New York: Basic Books.

Epstein, Jonathon. 1994. "Introduction: Misplaced Childhood: An Introduction to the Sociology of Youth and Their Music." In *Adolescents and Their Music: If It's Too Loud, You're Too Old*, edited by Epstein, Jonathon. New York and London: Garland Publishing, xiii to xxxiv.

Feagin, Joe R., and Hernán Vera. 1995. *White Racism: The Basics.* New York: Routledge.

Fear. 1985. *More Beer.* El Segundo, CA: Restless Records, 72039-1.

Fenster, Mark. 1992. "The Articulation of Difference and Identity in Alternative Popular Music Practice." Ph.D. diss., University of Illinois at Urbana-Champaign.

Foner, Philip S. (Editor). 1995. *The Black Panthers Speak.* New York: Da Capo Press.

Foucault, Michel. 1977. *Language, Counter-Memory, Practice.* Ithaca: Cornell University Press.

Franklin, Curtis. 1996. "A Conversation with Duane and some of Sacto's finest," *Heckler Magazine*, www.heckler.com/4.2tw/duane.html, accessed October 25, 1997.

Freire, Paulo. 1970a. *Cultural Action for Freedom.* Cambridge: Harvard Educational Review.

___ 1970b. *Pedagogy of the Oppressed.* New York: Continuum.

___ 1998. *Teachers as Cultural Workers.* Boulder, CA: Westview.

Frith, Simon. 1982. *Sound Effects: Youth, Leisure, and the Politics of Rock 'n' Roll.* New York: Pantheon Books.

Gaines, Donna. 1991. *Teenage Wasteland: Suburbia's Dead End Kids.* New York: Pantheon Books.

Giroux, Henry A. 1983. *Theory and Resistance in Education.* South Hadley, MA: Bergin and Garvey.

Giroux, Henry A., and Roger Simon. 1989. "Popular Culture as a Pedagogy of Pleasure and Meaning." In *Popular Culture: Schooling and Everyday Life*, edited by Henry A. Giroux. New York, Westport, Connecticut, and London: Bergin & Garvey, 1–30.

Gramsci, Antonio. 1971. *Prison Notebooks.* Translated by Quintin Hoare and Geoffrey Nowell Smith. New York: International Publishers.

Grossberg, Lawrence, Cary Nelson, and Paula A. Treichler. 1992. *Cultural studies.* New York: Routledge.

Henry, Tricia. 1989. *Break all the rules: punk rock and the making of a style.* London: UMI Research Press.

Holsti, Ole E. 1969. *Content Analysis for the Social Sciences and Humanities.* Boston: Addison-Wesley.

Horton, Donald. 1957. "The Dialogue of Courtship in Popular Songs." *American Journal of Sociology* 52: 569–578.

Horton, Myles, and Paulo Freire, edited by Brenda Bell, John Gaventa, and John Peters. 1996. *We Make the Road by Walking: Conversations on Education and Social Change.* Philadelphia, PA: Temple University Press, 1996.

Jackson, Philip. 1968. *Life in Classrooms.* New York: Holt, Rinehart and Winston.

Kent, Tania. 1998. "Two reports highlight the growth of global poverty and ill-health," http://www.wsws.org/news/1998/sep1998/pov-s23.shtml, accessed October 10, 2003.

Keyes, Cheryl. 1993. "'We're More than a Novelty, Boys': Strategies of Female Rappers in the Rap Music Tradition." In *Feminist Messages: Coding in Women's Folk Culture,* edited by Joan Newlon Radner. Urbana and Chicago: University of Illinois Press, 203–220.

Kloby, Jerry. 1999. *Inequality, Power and Development: The Task of Political Sociology.* New York: Humanity Books.

Krippendorff, Klaus. 1980. *Content Analysis: An Introduction to Its Methodology.* Beverly Hills, CA: Sage.

L7. 1988. *L7.* Los Angeles: Epitaph.

Laclau, Ernesto, and Chantal Mouffe. 1985. *Hegemony and Socialist Strategy: Toward a Democratic Politics.* London: Verso Books.

Laing, Dave. 1985. *One Chord Wonders: Power and Meaning in Punk Rock.* Philadelphia: Open University Press.

Lard. 1997. *Pure Chewing Satisfaction.* San Francisco: Alternative Tentacles, Virus 199.

Leaving Trains, The. 1992. *The Lump in My Forehead.* Lawndale, CA: SST, 288.

Lerner, Gerda A. 1986. *The Creation of Patriarchy.* New York and Oxford: Oxford University Press.

Lewis, Andy. 1997. "Dead Kennedys." http://www.geocities.com/SunsetStrip/Club/5321/dk.html, accessed October 25.

London, Herbert. 1984. *Closing the Circle: A Cultural History of the Rock Revolution.* Chicago: Helson-Hall.

Lopez, Ian. 1996. *White by Law: The Legal Construction of Race.* New York: New York University Press, 1996.

Marx, Gary T., and Douglas McAdam. 1994. *Collective Behavior and Social Movements: Process and Structure.* Englewood Cliffs, NJ: Prentice Hall.

Marx, Karl, and Friedrich Engels. 1964. *The Communist Manifesto 1848.* New York: Washington Square Press.

McDonald, James R. 1987. "Suicidal Rage: An Analysis of Hardcore Punk Lyrics." *Popular Music and Society* 11, no. 3: 91–102.

McLaren, Peter. 1989. *Life in Schools.* New York: Longman.

McMichael, Philip. 2000. *Development and Social Change: A Global Perspective Second Edition.* Thousand Oaks, CA: Pine Forge Press.

Melman, Seymour. 1970. *Pentagon Capitalism: The Political Economy of War.* New York: McGraw-Hill.

Miles, Matthew B., and Michael A. Huberman. 1984. *Qualitative Data Analysis: A Sourcebook of New Methods*, Beverly Hills, CA: Sage Publications.

Minutemen. 1980. *Paranoid Time.* Lawndale, CA: SST, 028.

Mohan, Amy B., and Jean Malone. 1994. "Popular Music as a 'Social Cement': A Content Analysis of Social Criticism and Alienation in Alternative-Music Song Titles." In *Adolescents and Their Music: If It's Too Loud, You're Too Old*, edited by Jonathon S. Epstein. New York and London: Garland Publishing, 283–300.

Morthland, John. 1985. "Punked Out." *High Fidelity* 35, no. 1: 68–78.

Naples, Nancy A. 1998. "Women's Community Activism: Exploring the Dynamics of Politicization and Diversity." In *Community Activism and Feminist Politics: Organizing across Race, Class, and Gender*, edited by Nancy A. Naples. New York: Routledge, 327–349.

Neuman, Lawrence. 1994. *Social Research Methods: Qualitative and Quantitative Approaches.* Boston: Allyn and Bacon.

O'Hara, Craig. 1995. *The Philosophy of Punk: More Than Noise!* San Francisco: AK Press.

Okolo, Fr. Chukwudum Barnabas. 1974. *Racism—A Philosophic Probe.* Jericho, New York: Exposition Press.

Peters, Duane. 1999. "US Bombs" In *Vans Warped Tour Presents: Punk Rock Summer Camp*, Executive Producers K. Lyman, D. Eaton, and R. Roskin. Los Angeles, CA: Side One Dummy Recordings.

Peterson, Eric E. 1989. "Media Consumption and Girls Who Want to Have Fun." *Critical Studies in Mass Communication* 4: 37–50.

Plato. 1928. *The Republic.* Translated by Benjamin Jowett. New York: Scribner's.

Robbins, Ira. 1997. "Tragic Mulatto." *Trouser Press.* http://www.trouserpress.com/entry.php?a=tragic_mulatto, accessed October 25, 1997.

Rosenau, Pauline Marie. 1992. *Post-Modern and the Social Sciences: Insights, Inroads, and Intrusions.* Princeton, NJ: Princeton University Press.

Shakur, Assata. 1987. *Assata: An Autobiography.* Chicago: Lawrence Hill Books.

Shea, Brent Mack. 1972. "A Content Analysis of the Lyrics of American Popular Music from 1967 to 1970." Master's thesis. Binghamton: State University of New York.

Shor, Ira. 1992. *Empowering Education.* Chicago, IL: University of Chicago Press.

Simon, Roger, Don Dippo, and Arleen Schenke. 1991. *Learning Work: A Critical Pedagogy of Work Education.* New York: Bergin and Garvey.

Snow, D. A., and C. Phillips. 1980. "The Lofland-Stark conversion model: A critical reassessment." *Social Problems* 27: 430–447.

Stein, Arlene. 1997. "Sisters and Queers: The Decentering of Lesbian Feminism." In *The Gender/Sexuality Reader: Culture, History, Political Economy*, edited by Roger N. Lancaster and Micaela di Leonardo. New York: Routledge, 378–391.

Tatum, Beverly D. 1997. "*Why Are All the Black Kids Sitting Together in the Cafeteria?": And Other Conversations about Race.* New York: Basic Books.

Temple, Julien. 2000. *The Filth and the Fury: A Sex Pistols Film.* Burbank, CA: Warner Home Video.

Touraine, Alain. 1981. *The Voice and the Eye.* Cambridge: Cambridge University Press.

Tragic Mulatto. 1989. *Hot Man Pussy.* San Francisco: Alternative Tentacles, Virus 74.

Tribe 8. 1995. *Fist City.* San Francisco: Alternative Tentacles, Virus 156.

Union 13. 1997. *East Los Presents...* Los Angeles: Epitaph, 86494-1.

___ 1997. "Band's Bio." http://www.epitaph.com/, accessed October 25.

Virgo, Sabina. 1996. "The Criminalization of Poverty." In *Criminal Injustice: Confronting the Prison Crisis,* edited by Elihu Rosenblatt. Boston, MA: South End Press, 47–61.

Willis, Paul. 1977. *Learning to Labor: How Working Class Kids Get Working Class Jobs.* New York: Columbia University Press.

Willis, Wesley. 1995. *Wesley Willis Greatest Hits.* San Francisco: Alternative Tentacles, Virus 164.

Wink, Joan. 2000. *Critical Pedagogy: Notes from the Real World.* New York: Longman, Second Edition.

Zinn, Howard. 1980. *A People's History of the United States: 1492 to the Present.* New York: Harper & Row Publishers.

___ 1997. *A People's History of the United States.* New York: The New Press.

Index

Studies in the Postmodern Theory of Education

General Editors
Joe L. Kincheloe & Shirley R. Steinberg

Counterpoints publishes the most compelling and imaginative books being written in education today. Grounded on the theoretical advances in criticalism, feminism, and postmodernism in the last two decades of the twentieth century, Counterpoints engages the meaning of these innovations in various forms of educational expression. Committed to the proposition that theoretical literature should be accessible to a variety of audiences, the series insists that its authors avoid esoteric and jargonistic languages that transform educational scholarship into an elite discourse for the initiated. Scholarly work matters only to the degree it affects consciousness and practice at multiple sites. Counterpoints' editorial policy is based on these principles and the ability of scholars to break new ground, to open new conversations, to go where educators have never gone before.

For additional information about this series or for the submission of manuscripts, please contact:

Joe L. Kincheloe & Shirley R. Steinberg
c/o Peter Lang Publishing, Inc.
275 Seventh Avenue, 28th floor
New York, New York 10001

To order other books in this series, please contact our Customer Service Department:

(800) 770-LANG (within the U.S.)
(212) 647-7706 (outside the U.S.)
(212) 647-7707 FAX

Or browse online by series:

www.peterlangusa.com